Aquafacs

Adventures of a Commercial Diver

Christopher Lee

Copyright © 2019 by Christopher B. Lee

The events and conversations in this book have been set down to the best of the author's ability, although some names and details have been changed to protect the privacy of individuals.

All rights reserved. No part of this book may be reproduced or used in any manner without written permission of the copyright owner except for the use of quotations in a book review.

First hardback edition November 2019

Book edited by Erin E. Lee
Book design by Jonathan C. Lee

ISBN 978-1-7342748-0-6 (hardback)

Beneath the ocean the weights of the world fall away and the majesty of creation envelops all that surrounds you and sustains you.

--- Christopher Lee

ACKNOWLEDGEMENTS

To my lovely wife, Susan, for her love and support and especially for her enduring all the ups and downs on our wild ride throughout the years, Love and thanks!

To my children, Melissa, Mindy, Kristin, Lindsay, James and Jonathan who had a mystery man for a father, constantly traveling, missing countless events and milestones in your early years, I thank you for your understanding and hope you'll accept my heartfelt apology for not having been there. My singular regret to my career as a Commercial Diver. Time is like a thief, robbing us of the things that matter most. I can rationalize that the need to support the family was paramount, but at this stage of life, to defend that notion, I struggle at times internally.

To My Parents, James and Louise Lee, for standing by me through the tough times and supporting my decision to become a Commercial Diver I am eternally grateful.

To Charles and Dorothy Proctor along with Susan's Grandmother Pauline Allen, for their support and compassion, without which it would have been impossible to move forward following our return from California, my most sincere appreciation.

To my brother Jay for having joined the madness that would become Aquafacs. His vision and fearless pursuit of business helped lead to the successful formation of Aquafacs and started our first adventures to the Canary Islands. Sail on Jay Lee.

And my siblings, Scott, Dana, Greg and Jean Marie. I have to thank you all for being there through the years, and in playing parts along the way that have contributed to and been included in this book, thank you.

George Osgood, David Keefe, and Capt. Bernie Marciniak joined with Jay Lee to form the business bulwark of Aquafacs. Their experience and drive turned the dream that was Aquafacs into the reality that pioneered many underwater services that are still in practice today.

To Charles W , visionary and villain, without whom we might still be in business as Aquafacs today, thanks for the learning experience. The uncertain path of life is lit by strange events and common cause. At one time we all subscribed to the dream and drank the cool aid that would lead to deceit and the demise of Aquafacs.

To all my family and friends that encouraged me to put pen to paper to capture stories of a time long past. For their willingness to allow me to ramble on recounting the occasions as if they were just lived in my first-person narrative. My co-workers for the last twenty-two years, my friends and captive audience, I thank you all and promise to never again mention the world-famous beer drinking pigs at the Domino Club in St. Croix, unless of course, you ask.

The stories and events happened as a result of the actions and efforts of dozens of Professional Divers and support personnel. My special thanks to Arne Backlund and his Swedish friends that were instrumental in the development of Aquafacs technical capabilities. He and his wife Lucy have been longtime friends since our meeting in 1984. We still go fishing and have a beer together from time to time.

In life, we all soldier on and live our own adventures, to all of you that read this book I express my thanks and encourage you all to live your adventures without fear, for we have but one life to live...

SPECIAL ACKNOWLEDGEMENTS

EDITOR: Erin Lee, My Very Smart Daughter in Law

Erin did a phenomenal job smoothing out the rough edges and correcting the endless number of spelling, grammar and punctuation mistakes. Not only can I not thank her enough for the incredible effort, but this book would have never made it without her help and direction. Many Thanks and Hugs

TECHNICAL ASSISTANCE: Jonathan Lee, My Son

Somehow I missed the memo that writing a book is the easy piece of creating a book. If I had read it, I might have reconsidered writing it. Collecting the pages and turning them into a print ready book is a journey rife with pitfalls and confusing computer programs and that's just the beginning of a long process and the next step.

Jon worked diligently on this project and provided the skill to navigate all the complexities that the common man would find insurmountable. Great Job ! Many Thanks!

ASSISTANT TECHNICAL SUPPORT Thank you to my highly talented Granddaughter Chloe for your creative selections and supporting your father's nearly impossible task to bring form to chaos ! Love and Hugs.

CONTENTS

AUTHOR'S NOTE	XI
PROLOGUE	XIII
CHAPTER ONE: MARBLEHEAD – IN THE BEGINNING	1
CHAPTER TWO: THE EPIPHANY	12
CHAPTER THREE: THE OCEANS CALL	17
CHAPTER FOUR: GRADUATION – ON TO THE FIELD	27
CHAPTER FIVE: BOSTON RESTART	56
CHAPTER SIX: LUCK OF THE IRISH	66
CHAPTER SEVEN: THE CANARY ISLANDS	78
CHAPTER EIGHT: MARINE ENGINEERS	85
CHAPTER NINE: REALITY SETS IN	91
CHAPTER TEN: SPIN OF THE WHEEL	102
CHAPTER ELEVEN: VLCC MASSACHUSETTS	130
CHAPTER TWELVE: FLEETWIDE PROGRAM	135
CHAPTER THIRTEEN: WEST COAST IMPLEMENTATION	147
CHAPTER FOURTEEN: APL LAUNCHES FLEET PROGRAM	156
CHAPTER FIFTEEN: USCG BUSINESS	164
CHAPTER SIXTEEN: AMERADA HESS	173
CHAPTER SEVENTEEN: AEGIS CRUISERS	195
CHAPTER EIGHTEEN: TRAINING	221
CHAPTER NINETEEN: NEW ENGLAND AQUARIUM	226
CHAPTER TWENTY: SEALAND	243
CHAPTER TWENTY-ONE: STANDING OVATION	253
CHAPTER TWENTY-TWO: AQUAFACS	262
ABOUT THE AUTHOR	265
REFERENCES	267

AUTHOR'S NOTE

The stories within are all based on true events and written from my best recollections. The times and people mentioned along the way are mostly true individuals and named as such. There are some, where names have been changed to maintain privacy or to protect sources, as the Shipping Community is perhaps the most secretive business on the planet. I have taken liberty to write all the adventures from my perspective and as such, there are some that shared the times at Aquafacs that may have a slightly different view of events. All in all, it is a collection of stories written to entertain as well as document some of the wild adventures of Aquafacs and its improbable start.

Christopher Lee, DSD

AQUAFACS

ADVENTURES OF A COMMERCIAL DIVER

PROLOGUE ... My story

The unlikely events that would drive me from pursuing an education in Cambridge to an adventure filled career as a hard hat commercial diver seemed could only have been driven by divine intervention. This book is based on true stories and the amazing luck that would sweep me along like the tides that would rise and fall through my early years. Coincidence, timing and opportunity would take me on a long trail from Boston to LA in pursuit of a dream. This book spans the period between mid-1976 through mid-1989. The following stories are autobiographical in nature, however, there were many characters along the way that led to the incredible adventures and times that would become Aquafacs.

Boston and a handful of small towns, known as the North Shore, make up the early landscape for people and events that would eventually lead to the formation of Aquafacs, a remarkable story of a business startup, especially in the Commercial Diving business.

I've entertained friends and family with stories of travel and adventures long after I ended my diving career at age forty-two. During my twenty-two-year career in telecom, I enjoyed telling those stories and was encouraged to put pen to paper to capture the moments.

As for me, there are many who worked as commercial divers and far exceeded my qualifications, but my luck and stories, including Aquafacs, are special and mine to share.

From inception, Aquafacs was formed to provide underwater services for the large ships of the Maritime Community. What we had no way of knowing was how our first projects would be life changing and take us to the Canary Islands off the coast of Morocco. Two Supertankers sat in layup in Las Palmas and were the subject of our first venture as Aquafacs. We were naïve and fearless.

We knew nothing about the twelve-hundred-foot-long behemoths that plied the open oceans transporting crude oil back in the day. They made stops at ports near developed oilfields in places like the Middle East, North Sea and Alaska and delivered to the refineries that would supply the world's insatiable need for petroleum products; gasoline, diesel, jet fuel, and heating oil to name a few.

Supertankers were so big they were rarely seen by the public as they were simply too large to navigate coastal waters of most countries due to their length and deep draft. For me, Aquafacs began with a simple question. What is a Supertanker?

The stories in this book are all based on true events. Dialogs, limited for story telling purposes, attempt to paint the scenes in real time as close to the actual conversations as possible and are written per my recollections.

Along with the stories, details were added describing equipment and techniques used by me and my crews as commercial divers. Some of those details may seem to bog down a bit, but I felt it important to give the reader a better understanding of the complexities and dangers of the commercial diving field.

Every ship call was an adventure and having worked on hundreds of ships, the contents of this book are but a small fraction of the Aquafacs story. I was an active participant in all the actual diving stories. It would be impossible to write them all.

For me, the stories serve as a walk back in time during my career in marine construction and commercial diving. We weaved our way through the Reagan and Gorbechev years in the fast-changing world of the shipping and oil community. These were truly interesting times.

To develop some understanding and a foundation for my background, the story begins a few years before heading to LA with a glimpse of my life leading up to the wild ride that would become Aquafacs.

Members of my family played big parts along the way and it only makes sense to start with meeting the love of my life without whom none of this is likely to have happened.

CHAPTER ONE

MARBLEHEAD - IN THE BEGINNING

I came into this world number five of six children to an Irish Catholic Mother and Methodist Father in 1953.

My father's family arrived in Virginia from England in 1642. Richard Lee, a tax collector for the King, was not a very popular guy. In the 1700s, Richard Henry Lee was the most notable and earliest family member my Grandmother, Margaret Scott Lee, born in the 1880's, spoke of as the source of our lineage. Richard and his brother Francis Lightfoot Lee both signed the Declaration of Independence and were the source of immense pride for my Grandmother as she told her story to us at a young age. Outside of that, she never much spoke of the long family heritage. I'd find out much later why. The Civil War.

George Wythe
Richard Henry Lee
Th Jefferson
Benj Harrison
Th Nelson jr
Francis Lightfoot Lee
Carter Braxton

Our family home was in Marblehead. When I was old enough to be aware of the world around me, I'd run to my mother and say, "Mommy, I need one of those. Scottie has one." I'm guessing this started as soon as I could talk.

My mother would always say, "OK, but you'll have to wait until my ship comes in."

"Great," I'd think, imagining a ship full of my mother's things heading this way with my new bike or whatever it was I needed at the time.

Somehow, her ship never seemed to come in, and my bike never much got past a beat-up hand me down. When would my ship ever come in? ... I can't help but think this was the subconscious source of my life-long quest for my ship to come in.

Fast forward to 1976.

At age 23, in the summer of 1976, the Bicentennial Year, my good friend and scuba diving buddy, Mike Walsh and I worked together in construction. So it was, that after work on a Friday night in the middle of June, we went out on the town to a place called the Harbor House, a popular Disco Night Club halfway to Boston from Marblehead. It was a couple of weeks before the 4th of July and we had a mission. Split up and track down the two best looking girls in the place, and then meet back at the bar.

It was on the late side when we hit the Disco, and having no lack of confidence, we set out and scoured the club. Having any hope of meeting girls at that time of night required moving fast and a little luck. The flashing light show, pounding music and famous ball of confusion painted the club with the party scene so well remembered with the disco days.

There were several hundred people in the club, and in the disco, there was plenty of color, funky clothes and leisure suits. Neither Mike nor I had time to change and think about fashion at that time of night. We decided to take our chances, especially with how great all the girls looked dressed up for the disco scene. After twenty minutes or so of scouting, we rounded back and spied a couple of brunettes hanging together near the bar. Both were incredibly attractive.

We introduced ourselves and were happily surprised that they were approachable and friendly. They said they'd been there all night waiting to meet people and have a little fun. To their dismay, nobody had shown any interest or even said hello. They were happy and maybe relieved that Mike and I came along. My guess, they were probably too hot for the disco losers that didn't even bother to try. Our good luck.

Our mission was working. The younger of the two was probably underage for alcohol, but she looked great. The older of the pair appeared to be of legal age and had a classy, beautiful look. The two girls were exactly what we were looking for and measured up as the best-looking duo in the crowd. We had a great time hanging out, despite our inappropriate dress, and we closed the club. Time to go. We left with the girls' names, phone numbers, and the promise for a follow-up.

I found myself attracted to the older of the girls we just met. Her name was Susan. She was going through a painful time, in the process of getting divorced. The younger of the two was Susan's younger, much younger, sister-in-law who had coaxed her to go out to the Disco that night.

I thought there was something special about Susan. I would find out later that she was voted most attractive in her high school class in Ipswich. Her sister-in-law was in fact underage with a fake ID the night we met. No surprise there. I planned to call Susan and see about setting up a date.

1976: The Bicentennial

Everyone was planning something special for the bicentennial. We were no exception and planned a special event, a harbor cruise and barbeque in Marblehead the day before the 4th.

Except for the locals and a few historians, most did not know how wrapped up in the founding of the nation Marblehead as a town had been. A life size painting of the 'Spirit of '76' by Archibald Willard hangs in the town hall. The fife and drum and young flag bearer marching in battle is one of the most recognizable paintings of the American Revolution.

It is said that French General Lafayette (Marie-Joseph Paul Yves Roch Gilbert du Motier, Marquis de **Lafayette**,) friend and close ally of George Washington, trained the local militia on the grounds of what is now Abbot Hall.

The locals say it was men from Marblehead who rowed Washington across the Delaware on that frigid Christmas Eve in 1776, where he defeated and captured the Prussian mercenaries in Trenton, New Jersey. Some say that was a legend, but it is accepted fact by most in Marblehead.

My oldest brother Jay lived up the Danvers River, not far from Marblehead, and had a thirty-foot-long steel hull barge tied up out back. It had an eight-foot-wide plywood deck with blue indoor-outdoor carpet and handrails for safety, or more like a corral to keep anyone from becoming a 'man overboard.' This had a high probability with all the beer and alcohol consumed while the barge plied the waters of Salem Bay. The barge looked great and ready to go after a little touch-up and paint.

Being the bicentennial, it had to have a large flag to fly and pole to handle it. The pole was a serious challenge as the flag we planned to fly was twelve feet long. With a little help, I found an extruded aluminum pipe and fabricated a thirty-foot-tall flagpole with simple trucking gear. With the help of our bicentennial crew, I mounted it on the aft deck of the barge. It looked amazing! The flag would fly.

We hoped to entertain up to fifty people as guests and passengers for our harbor cruise and barbeque on Saturday the 3rd of July in celebration of the 4th in Marblehead. We rounded up everything. Four full kegs of beer, piles of chicken and steak for the grill, and even a portable outhouse, personally handcrafted by me. Complete with halfmoon door and pitched roof, it would be landed on the beach when we finished the harbor cruise and made landfall for the barbeque.

Brown's Island, a small island in Little Harbor just east of Peaches Point in Marblehead, would be the venue for the beach party and barbeque following the cruise. This was going to be an historic event. Susan would be my guest, if she agreed and dared to go.

I called her for the first time early in the week that followed our Disco encounter and invited her out to dinner at the Landing Restaurant on the waterfront in Marblehead. She accepted and agreed to meet me there on Saturday night.

The harbor cruise was fast approaching, and the 4th was the following Sunday. We enjoyed a great meal on the outside deck overlooking Marblehead harbor, and after a while I invited her to the upcoming barge excursion. Not sure what she thought after filling her in on the details, but she agreed to make it. We finished up our first date, and after a short stroll around the wharf, Susan departed. Less than one week to go before the cruise and barbeque.

Too bad she missed the '1976 Great Race' earlier in June. My brother Greg and I were made famous having made the Boston Sunday Globe following the Race thanks to a fine piece of back yard engineering. With dogged determination to compete and a newly constructed paddle wheel canoe, we were ready to go. Ah, the Great Race.

The Bicentennial festivities started early in 1976. For Marblehead, the Great Race would be one of the highlights leading up to the bicentennial celebrations on the 4th of July. The Great Race itself was an event started years earlier by way of a bar room bet at Maddie's in Marblehead. The bet was that a man could paddle a canoe from Watertown, a town located down the Charles River from Boston, and across the waters to Marblehead faster than a man could run or walk the distance.

The rules were simple. The contestants would start at the same ungodly pre-dawn hour in Watertown. Either by canoe or running, they would race to Maddie's in Marblehead. Upon crossing the finish line, the Race Committee would commiserate and decide the first arrival would be disqualified for cheating, figuring that would be the only way to win against such odds.

The second finisher would then be declared winner. Once again to be reviewed by the Race Committee, only to be disqualified for cheating, being loudly proclaimed by the first disqualified contestant and on and on it would go.

In the end there would never be a formally declared winner of the Great Race, but the party was on. Down on State Street in Marblehead, the beer flowed like water.

In preparation for the 1976 Great Race I went to work and invented a two-man paddle wheel canoe. It was a contraption built out of the workings of a ten-speed bike. It had an axle that straddled the canoe and held a paddle wheel on each end. Constructed out of short cross-sectional pieces of the same extruded aluminum pipe used for the flagpole, it would have the strength to hold the paddles.

The hubs were bored out to fit six paddles on each of the two wheels and epoxied into place. Both wheels were then screwed and epoxied to each end of the axle after the gear assembly was welded halfway across. The paddle wheel axle assembly, gears and peddles were centered up and set slightly forward on the canoe for a person to power the paddle wheels.

By sitting in position on the floor of the canoe and propped up to a comfortable position, the craft could be easily peddle powered. With six paddles on each wheel, it required much testing to determine how deep in the water the paddles should go without taking too big a bite. The goal was to power the canoe efficiently and not wear out the guy pedaling the machine.

The second critical part of the contraption was a makeshift tiller with an over the top handle made of flexible copper tubing fitted to one paddle with a fixed hull attachment for ease of steering. One man peddled while the second navigated. After much trial and error, we had our canoe finely tuned. Not only did it work, it looked amazing, and it was fast.

The day of the race, we transported the canoe fully assembled and entered the water in Watertown ready to go. When the starting cannon fired, we left the starting line and everyone in our wake. Try as they might, nobody could keep up with us other than an Indian war canoe with over a dozen people paddling. Guess the hull speed of a much larger canoe could best us, but we matched their twelve paddles and rocked our canoe nearly reaching planing speed. The difference was that we could endure the pace, but could that war canoe? Didn't matter.

True to traditions of the race and undeniability of regular cheating, we had a strategy. We peddled our way to the end of the Charles. Greg and I having proved the genius of our design and with an abundance of caution decided to portage the contraption by motor vehicle to the Nahant causeway, the final leg over water from Nahant to Marblehead.

Our accomplice, Anneke Carter, was waiting for us near the Museum of Science by the locks at the end of the Charles River. She had been drafted to join the crew in our mission for the paddle wheel canoe and navigated the traffic flawlessly, meeting us as planned. We loaded out and drove to the Nahant causeway, awaiting the sighting of the first canoes inbound from Boston. Seemed like forever before the other canoes arrived, and we launched on the last leg to Deveraux Beach. We needed to reserve our energy for the beach party to come.

I was peddling the canoe with my brother Greg at the tiller. We were quite a sight. With six paddles on each side, we painted two red, two white and two blue. We were the picture of true Patriotic spirit. Red white blue, red white blue, red white blue the paddles gleamed as we finished and pulled our craft through the surf on Deveraux Beach.

A Boston Globe reporter was there who photographed us just as we pulled in and dragged the canoe and our contraption out of the water. So, there we were, front page of the Boston Sunday Globe, the Bicentennial. We would be immortal, one for the ages in Marblehead in 1976, now buried in the archives somewhere.

Time for the Harbor Cruise

By Saturday the 3rd of July, we were ready for the next adventure. The harbor cruise and barbeque, loaded out and flag flying proud, was set to sail. The crowd gathered at Commercial Street Wharf in Marblehead. We figured fifty people would max out the loading on the barge. Not officially, but we didn't want to make the Globe again with a disaster at sea story.

Susan arrived along with the rest of the invited guests. The total was just a couple heads short of the fifty estimated. With the crowd on board, we cast off and began our harbor excursion.

The barge was no speedboat. It was powered by a single twenty-five horsepower outboard and strained to make headway as we left the dock. After a short distance, we discovered that the water displacement of the hull and the load on deck were not too far apart. In fact, the freeboard was no more than six to eight inches depending on the direction the barge listed. We had failed to factor in the weight of the four kegs, ice, food, and portable outhouse.

Now underway, our passengers would shift from side to side to view the sights of Marblehead harbor, and the barge would begin to list in the direction of the crowd. Could be a problem. Given enough of a shift to one side or the other we might risk a catastrophic roll over.

We had to make an urgent request. I called out "Please pay attention to the Captain Mike Walsh at the wheel. If we begin to list too much in either direction the Captain will ask you to shift right or shift left. Please shift slightly to the other side of the barge." The announcement seemed to work. With a delicate barge ballet, a manageable balance was achieved.

Spectacle that we were, the Marblehead Police boat spotted us as we approached the mouth of the harbor. He didn't dare get too close but hailed the barge. "Show me your life jackets," he said.

We really hadn't considered the need for safety equipment, like we might need fifty life jackets. Everyone looked around and the Captain of the barge called out, "Roll up your towels or beach bags and hold them over your head!"

The crowd followed the direction, all laughing as they held up their 'life jackets.' The Captain of the Police boat just shook his head and slowly turned away without shutting us down. Close call! We continued to Brown's Island and our party to come.

We had a fun time. I still remember the cry from the crew of the barge after beaching on Brown's Island, "Lower the sh*t house!" We needed the portable to keep the neighbors from complaining about our party watering the vegetation on Brown's Island. I'm sure Susan was impressed by our thorough planning. She may have had her doubts about her new friends, but it didn't seem to faze her. A good sign.

Better Together

Not long after all the excitement of the bicentennial and dating for a little while, Susan and I decided to move in together. By the fall of 1978, we were living in Salem, Massachusetts. Working construction during the day, I would travel by train after work to Cambridge for night school.

Harvard offered an opportunity through their extension program to attain a degree. It allowed me to establish a routine that might pay off some day. Harvard made sense. I had an interest in the Diplomatic Corp and it could be a good path to follow. With no real set goals other than 'you have to start somewhere' I plodded along. My path at Harvard just might get me somewhere.

CHAPTER TWO

THE EPIPHANY

One Friday afternoon in early October 1978, I was back at the Landing Bar and Grill on the waterfront in Marblehead. The Landing was well known for cheap beers during Happy Hour and a good place to hang out with friends. It was the same place I had taken Susan on our first date. I had gone there to practice playing darts, and as a member of the Landing Team in the Minuteman Dart League, it was imperative that you practice and hone your skills at darts as well as drink beer. The hoisting of beer mugs was good exercise for the lower arm muscles needed to fire the darts with any hope of hitting a bullseye, or anything else for that matter.

The Landing had been one of my favorite watering holes in Marblehead long before meeting Susan. It was located next to Graves Yacht Yard where in the year Spring of 1977, Ted Turner kept his redesigned 12-Meter sailboat COURAGEOUS. Turner was in town tuning up his boat to compete against Ted Hood for the honor of defending the Americas Cup in 1977. Turner's boat had originally been owned and sailed by Ted Hood to successfully defend the Americas Cup in 1974. Turner bought and refitted the COURAGEOUS and was there to win, if I remember correctly. COURAGEOUS was fitted with the first wing keel design. The two Teds now battled it out for the honor of depending the Cup in 1977.

Hood, a Marblehead resident, World Class sailmaker and down the street neighbor from where I grew up, was favored to win. He put up his new 12-Meter entry INDEPENDENCE to represent. He kept her tied up at the dock behind his house across the harbor from the Landing on Marblehead Neck. Who would defend the Cup? We knew it would be a Ted.

Turner had famously spent afternoons at the Landing buying the whole bar rounds after long days sailing against Hood in the Americas Cup trials. He had a gigantic tractor trailer with a satellite dish parked behind the Landing where you could step outside with a drink and watch a live sports feed of the teams he owned from Atlanta on a huge screen. This was something special. I enjoyed the sailing carnival and drank a bunch of free beer. Turner would go on driving COURAGEOUS and bested Hood in the trials. INDEPENDENCE with Hood at the helm would never perform well enough to become the defender.

Turner would go on to victory in '77 in a 4-0 series over Australia. I remember he had a young guy, Robbie Doyle, custom make his sails for COURAGEOUS, which was probably a crucial factor in Turner's victory. Robbie was a local from Marblehead. I remembered him from my days as a kid hanging around the Pleon Yacht Club, a junior yacht club associated with the EYC (Eastern Yacht Club) in Marblehead. He went on to become, like his mentor Hood, a World Class sailmaker. I see Doyle sails everywhere I go on the waterfront these days. Colorful times, Marblehead had always been a big sailing town and where I'd develop my love for the ocean and the Landing.

So, it was in October 1978, in the Landing playing darts that I noticed the front door open, and in strode Patrick

Mulroy. Patrick had been a good friend through the high school years and even before that going back to Troop 32 Boy Scout days. Hadn't seen him since high school some six years earlier.

He gave me a big grin and said, "Hey Man. What's going on? Haven't seen you in years, since high school." Seemed like a long time ago.

I shook his hand and said, "Not much. How 'bout you?"

Patrick said, "I just got back from diving school and stopped in for a couple of cold ones before hitting the road."

"Diving school? Like scuba diving?" I asked.

"No. Like hard hats, hoses, compressors and all that kind of thing," he said. Having been a scuba diver myself and chasing lobsters around for years, no one ever said anything about commercial diving as an occupation. I'd never heard of such a thing. Doctors, Lawyers, Firemen, Commercial Divers?

I asked Patrick, "How'd you ever get into that?"

"Stevie Richards told me about it. He got into it a couple years ago and works for a company called Atlantic Divers. When I got out of diving school, he got me a job working for Atlantic. I have to leave tomorrow for Portland to report for work."

"Portland Maine?" I asked.

"No, Oregon." *You gotta be kidding*, I thought. Richards was a couple of years ahead of us in school.

This sounded way more interesting than where I'd been heading. Night school at Harvard was a long slog with an uncertain future. I needed to hear more. This could be just the clear path I'd hope to find. I loved chasing lobsters around and was comfortable in the water. That was underwater...

I asked Patrick, "What are you going to be doing out there?"

"I don't know," he said, "but Stevie said I can make a pile of money working at Atlantic. Could be a couple hundred grand a year if I keep after it. I had to give it a shot. Couldn't pass up the chance! Besides the certification training didn't take long, only four months or so."

I stood there in mild shock. I was pretty good in the water, and scuba diving was no big deal. What did he just say about the pay? Nobody I knew was making anything near that. In fact, most people, professional or not, weren't even close. Now you're up there with Doctors and Lawyers kind of pay. This was after all 1978...

He could see the confused look on my face and continued, "I know," he said, "sounds too good to be true, but when Stevie told me about it, I dropped everything and signed up. The place is called Commercial Diving Center out in Wilmington, California. When I went there, I got my Air and Mixed Gas Certification. He said to call him when I got out. I did, so here I am on the way to Portland tomorrow."

We had a few more beers and joked about the good old days, then off he went. I was left shaking my head and needing more details about this whole commercial diving thing. Our chance encounter left me with a strong need to consider that there might be something better than hanging around the Landing in Marblehead and slogging my way through night school. Time to find out more about that school in LA.

Thinking about it later, I had to chuckle. Patrick's nickname in high school, believe it or not, was Mud Shark. Mine had been Buffalo Bill for my long hair and scraggly beard. Rollie, our bus driver for the high school hockey team, tagged me with that one. Thanks a bunch.

At that time, I was considered a bit of a freak of nature. Born and raised in an affluent setting, my appearance didn't fit the image of high school jocks known for crew cuts and following all the rules, clearly that was not me. I was just happy to play goalie. Nobody cared that I could sail or swing a pretty mean tennis racket.

That nick name stuck with me for years beyond high school. I can't tell you how many times I heard, "Hey Buffalo Bill!" Not that I cared. Guess it was OK to be remembered. After all I was a pretty good tennis player and helped Marblehead win their first State Championship in any sport in their long history.

CHAPTER THREE

THE OCEANS CALL

The following Monday I called Commercial Diving Center to request information and a registration package. When it arrived, I calculated how much it would cost to get through the Air and Mixed Gas program with special underwater burning and welding plus explosives training add-ons. I lobbied family and friends to raise the money and left to join Class D-102 three weeks later, leaving Susan behind in Salem to hold down the fort, a tough assignment for which I would pay the price later.

The week before leaving for Commercial Diving school there was a birthday party in Old Town Marblehead for one of my friends. There were a bunch of people going to the Smith Sister's house. It would be a terrific opportunity to say goodbye before heading out to God knows where. Turned out to be quite a party, lots of alcohol and plenty of mother nature by the pungent smell. Turns out, one of my best friends and longtime acquaintances was there, Robert 'Bo' Johnson. I hadn't seen Bo in several years and was surprised that he was getting ready to attend Maine Maritime Academy and pursue a career in the Merchant Marines. He said his goal was to get a degree, training and sea time to work his way up to be a ship Captain. This would be a lengthy process as graduating from Maine Maritime would qualify him to start as an officer on deck of a commercial ship as third mate, the first step and bottom rung of a long ladder to make Captain. In the end, a great paying job.

I told Bo how our mutual pal Patrick Mulroy had just educated me on the whole commercial diving thing. We continued to drink and debate the merits of a protracted career pursuing his dream of Captain versus my accelerated plan to conquer the same ocean from a little different perspective, with the potential for adventure and quick riches.

It was approaching that special last call time of night. We decided to do a toast and poured a couple of brandies in oversized snifters. We clinked our glasses together with a toast for success when my glass slid out of my chest-high hand and dropped four feet to the hardwood floor below.

To our shock and amazement, the oversized crystal snifter hit the floor landing flat on its base. Not only did it not shatter but didn't spill a drop! We looked at each other and laughed out loud. Clearly this was a sign from above. We were both ready for lift off... And off we went. That was in late 1978. I wouldn't hear of his progress until twelve years later in 1990, an amazing coincidence at a bar in the bowels of the Caribbean.

Time to go. Driving an old truck cross country to LA from Salem, I found the school in Wilmington, California, dubbed the 'Heart of the Harbor.' I had a better slogan that rhymes, change the 'H' in heart to an 'F.' The place had a strange smell. A combination of gas and oil fumes that were generated by the local refineries and cat food from the tuna canneries on Terminal Island. The combination left me feeling a little queasy until I got accustomed to it.

At the school, they posted housing opportunities and general information for new arriving students. The place was in revolving session, and there were students wandering around. I had no idea what they were up to, but I would soon find out. Class D-102 was due to start the next day.

When our class assembled first thing on that Monday morning, the Director of the School, Jim Joiner, introduced himself and his staff of instructors, He said, "Take a good look around. By the time this class graduates there will only be half of you remaining."

The director went on, "Of the half of you that will graduate, only four of you will ever go on to work as Commercial Divers. After a year that number drops to two, and after five years, less than one of you will still be employed in any capacity in the industry as far as we can figure. So good luck!" Sounded like you needed more than luck. I doubted his statistics. Maybe that was his way of inspiring people.

With those numbers, why would anybody go through this and spend the time and money with little hope for any kind of work prospect? I guess for those tough enough (or dumb enough) to complete the course, he was making sure there were no great expectations of where this might lead. Seemed like an odd introduction and certainly not what I'd call a great motivational speech. Whatever his issues were, I had no doubt about what Patrick had said and was sure I would be the exception to his stats. My determination was all I needed and had plenty of it. I was sure that I would be there at the end.

The class had started with thirty-two members. The group included a young Vietnamese guy, Son Ha, a former SVN Air Force pilot deemed a hero for flying a fighter jet out of harm's way before the fall of Saigon.

The training turned out to be rigorous and the equipment completely foreign to me. All the hoses, diving helmets and everything else we were expected to train with all looked well used. Not sure if that was good or bad, but I hoped they all worked. The training was a combination of classroom and hands-on. I guessed the equipment and exercises must have been geared for the few who would ever actually make it to the field.

We started with scuba drills. Why would we be doing these for commercial training? Might be part of a weeding out plan. Like a clever way to cull the class, removing those that didn't belong from the start. They did say the class would be shrinking to half. The scuba drills ended up washing out a handful of students who didn't realize they were supposed to be proficient in scuba before taking the next step to commercial diving. Hard to believe. Who knows, ultimately the school may have saved a life or two along the way, theirs or others that might have depended on their training and skills to survive.

As for the drills, we worked in teams of two in a low visibility, fifteen-foot-deep by ten-foot diameter tank where we performed ditch and don drills, removing and then dressing back into our scuba gear. As luck would have it, I was teamed up with Son Ha. Little did I know what fun this was going to be. He spoke English, so there were no real communication issues. Well, not as far as language goes anyway.

I would go first. He would dress in with scuba gear, enter the tank and act as safety diver while I worked on my drill. When I had suited up and Son Ha was in place, the instructor gave me the thumbs up, and I dropped to the bottom of the tank. The visibility was bad, so I was careful to remove my tank, weight belt, fins and finally set my mask carefully on the pile under the end of my weight belt to make it easy to retrieve before ascending.

In this setting while wearing a wet suit and having left your fins and weight belt on the bottom, one had to kick hard to get back down and reach his equipment. When you got back down, you had to grab your mask, slinging your weight belt across your lap, find and stuff your regulator in your mouth to breathe, clear your mask, and tighten things up. Before you could finish you had to put your fins on and then rise to the surface. All was to be performed as a timed exercise and not that difficult except for the wet suit buoyancy thing and lousy water visibility.

Turns out, while Son Ha was thrashing around in that lousy visibility, he kicked over my carefully placed pile and knocked my mask to the far side of the tank, unbeknownst to me. So off I went to complete the task only to find my gear strewn all over the place and my mask missing. I had my hand on the tank, so air was no issue. Took a little time to feel around and find my weight belt while kicking and seemingly standing on my head due to the wet suit buoyancy. Laying the belt across my lap and now having air and buoyancy control, I was able to grope around for my mask and fins. I found a fin, then the mask which I promptly donned and cleared, before going on to find my second fin. I was pissed.

When I surfaced and got out of the tank, the instructor was laughing his ass off. He had seen Son Ha kick my gear all over the place through the port hole on the side of the tank.

He said, "Lee, you failed the time trial. But don't worry, I won't hold that against you. As a matter of fact, I was pretty impressed you hadn't popped up and asked for a redo. I thought, *Great. Thanks for your confidence.*

It was now Son Ha's turn. Now I was the safety diver and careful to make sure he had everything he needed and in fact handed him his mask when he first got back down to his gear to make sure we didn't have delays. I just wanted to get through this nonsense. This was supposed to be commercial diving school, and this exercise didn't seem like training. Son Ha, from what I heard, sounded like he needed and had earned a break.

I finally felt Class D-102 was about to begin. Turns out they had another special training that might be likely to weed out a few others along the way. It was called heavy gear. Think of an old Navy Diver with a giant helmet, solid brass breast plate, and full body canvas suit. It requires wearing a ninety-pound weight belt with cross straps and D ring for air umbilical hose attachment and lead-weighted boots. If worn correctly, heavy gear could provide a reliable, albeit archaic, diving system with good buoyancy control and a dry suit to work in. Even with all the lead, the suit provided good mid-water control and was worn with no fins. This was something special but hopefully nothing actually needed in the 'real' world.

For me, not being that tall, I had an immediate challenge. When I looked at the suit, it seemed like it was seven feet tall. We had a brief classroom session before hands-on training and on to the tank to give this a try. The instructor said, "when you get dressed, make sure your jock strap from the weight belt is so tight your crotch hurts."

When properly dogged down over the breast plate it was hard to stand and felt like it squeezed the family jewels flat in the crotch of that canvas suit. He said, "Hey don't worry about it. When you get in the water, you'll be light as a feather," as he laughed at his own joke. Clearly there was more to this and he was holding back. Some of the class felt this was a form of underwater torture.

I watched while one of my fellow classmates was ready to go and climbed down the ladder. He entered the training tank and sank directly to the bottom, ten to twelve feet, while yelling, "take up my slack."

Should have paid better attention to the brief classroom training, I thought. His suit flooded. They had described in class how to control the air flow and buoyancy thing. Seals had to be right and tight.

My turn. I guess Son Ha and I were now joined at the hip, and he served as my tender for heavy gear in tank training. The key, I figured, was to make sure your suit and breast plate were well attached and tightened enough to make a good seal on the suit.

The top of the breast plate was threaded. A quarter turn twist of the helmet would make a watertight seal on a leather gasket between the breast plate ring and helmet. If done right, along with the weight belt and boots, you should have a fighting chance not to make a fool of yourself.

I carefully directed Son Ha to help with donning the gear and properly torqueing the breast plate seals. It was time to twist on the helmet, climb in, and try this stuff out. When I let go of the ladder, I had enough air in the suit and seemed to be buoyant enough with the air flow gently hissing behind my head. I had it well adjusted and blowing gently.

There is a button inside the helmet above and behind your ear which they call a chin button, go figure. When you depress the button with your head, it exhausts air from the suit. This functions along with the free flow of air to allow for control of the buoyancy.

Being a free flow system, air in your suit allows you to rise or sink by maintaining the correct volume and striking a balance of incoming and outgoing airflow. Done right, you can remain comfortable and neutrally buoyant. Great. I got this.

Suddenly, while I was adjusting the ancient equipment to help offset the discomfort where the instructor assured us would be no problem, my belt slipped and must have lost a notch somehow. My helmet rode up, bashed my chin and nearly sucked my head through the breast plate.

Son Ha had failed to properly pin the belt to the correct hole and left me hanging. This was bad news, as I could no longer reach and depress the chin button to exhaust the air. My head slid below the reach. The suit began to blow up like a balloon. Guess he at least got the suit seals right. Before the suit fully inflated, leaving me a balloon man needing to be rescued, I was just able to reach and turn off my air supply valve, allowing the suit to slowly deflate while I made my way back to the ladder. Had to be the only time in my life that being deflated was a good thing.

The humiliation, on the other hand, was becoming a little too regular hanging around with Son Ha. This time, however, was my fault for not having double-checked the straps and belts, relying on my tender. Lesson learned.

The good thing was I had controlled the air flow and handled the situation as well as could be expected. As anybody who has ever trained or worn this equipment can tell you, the incident caused a major bruise and scrape to my chin as my head and face were literally being sucked inside the breast plate.

There were many things I learned at that school, but clearly, the trade was far from anything I had imagined. I only hoped that I'd gained enough training to survive. I did finish first in my class, despite Son Ha and a few other bumps along the way. That might count for something.

The explosives training with famed underwater blaster Jerry Brower leading the class was my favorite part of the school training. Jerry invented the BROCO rod commonly used for underwater burning of steel or anything else in the way. Being an oxygen lance, it would cut anything, including concrete. Any readers familiar with the trade will appreciate Jerry's contributions.

We had hands on training with live explosives to include C4, tri-mix and shape charges. Proper use of det cord and learning the dos and don'ts of handling high explosives were the focus of our training. Couldn't help but notice Jerry was missing a couple of fingers when I shook his hand when we first met.

Each of us were given the explosive components and tasked with preparing live shots on large inch thick, three by three-foot steel plates. We followed instructions for each shot, and after inspection by our instructor, moved to a safe distance. Jerry's helper, Al Daratany, would holler, "Fire in the hole!" Then boom, the blast created shock waves at our location.

It was a momentous day out on the range. When it was time to go, Jerry asked us to prepare our final shot. The plan was to use any and all materials that were left and then using det cord, tie all the components together. Jerry would judge the best of the four teams' efforts.

My team was clearly more creative in our plan and decided to see if we could balance the remaining materials while tying a string together under the four corners to see if we could blow that plate out of the depressed ground area where we set our charges. How far in the air could we launch that three by three steel plate? It had to be creative so the det cord connection from the wimpy looking arrangement on top of the plate didn't show the real fire power below.

After Jerry inspected the four teams work, we headed back to the safe zone. Al called out, "Fire in the hole!" and then BOOM. This time our plate blew straight up in the air. It looked like slow motion as the plate rose up and up and kept on going...

Holy Shit! Jerry Brower was pissed. "Who the hell fired that shot?" he yelled.

We had to fess up. He went on and on about how dangerous it was, and the plate looked like it exceeded 1,000 feet and put small aircraft in harm's way. I doubt it got higher than 500. Although, we were so far out in the desert that there wasn't a small aircraft for a hundred miles. It was a real verbal beat down.

As we rolled up our gear, Al Daratany came by and said, "great shot!" and then walked off. Al was not only helping Jerry out but was on Jim Joiner's staff at CDC.

CHAPTER FOUR

GRADUATION – ON TO THE FIELD

At the graduation ceremony for Class D-102, a special representative from Oceaneering International was introduced and announced how pleased he was that the whole class had been offered to come to work for Oceaneering. If you were ready, they were there to hire immediately and invited everyone to sign up. Seemed like a good idea, instant employment.

After the brief ceremony, I was pulled aside by Al Daratany. He told me to hold back and not sign up. He had been a good instructor, and I valued his opinion. It wouldn't be much of a surprise if Al was former CIA or some sort of black ops military guy based on his stories. He was especially proud of blowing bridges in Southeast Asia a decade or so earlier.

He said, "You've got what it takes kid. If you go with that bunch, you'll spend at least two years as a diver's tender, and the only water you'll see is on crew boats or from standing on a pier somewhere holding someone else's hose. Go see my pal Bob down at the Piledrivers Hall and tell him I sent you."

I said "Al, these guys are ready to hire us now and put us to work. I need the money and can use the time at Oceaneering to figure things out."

Al laughed, "By the time you figure things out, the real opportunities will be gone. So, you might as well just go home to that barstool you came from. At least then you can brag how you're a big bad Commercial Diver and see if anybody will buy you a drink."

Wow, that was harsh, but I couldn't help but think he'd seen it all before with newbies just getting their feet wet, or not. Hey, I knew my friends were still sitting around playing darts and drinking beer at the Landing in Marblehead. They'd be there when I got back, but that I didn't want to go home by being stupid...

I took Al's advice and went down the street to see his pal Bob at the Piledrivers Union. The Union Hall was a small, freestanding building and had a reception area with well-worn looking chairs. I went to the reception window and was met by a very friendly older woman with thick glasses and a nice smile. I asked if Bob Bradley was in. She said he was and asked me to take a seat while she tracked him down. In the lobby there were all sorts of enlarged photos that showed construction action on bridges and waterfront piers. They all showed cranes with piledriving equipment and the men at work. Really big looking stuff. Made me a little uncomfortable looking at the scale of all these projects.

A few minutes later, the door at the other end of the lobby opened, and it was Bob Bradley. He was a heavy-set guy with that weathered look you'd only get from working outdoors for some long period of time. "Hello there, you must be Chris," he said. "I'm Bob Bradley. Heard you might be coming by. Got a call from Al Daratany over at that diving school. He said you were top in your class and just might be the kind of guy we need. Things are about to get really busy."

I told him Al had really twisted my arm to stick around while the rest of my class all went to work in the Gulf for

Oceaneering International. Bob didn't seem too impressed by the whole class heading there.

He surprised me when he said," I hear there's little more than a bunch of Coon Ass down there in the Gulf. Now why the hell would anyone want to go there?"

With that, we started a conversation about the Piledrivers Union, and he gave me a brief history lesson about the trade. I listened to Bob's speech about the Piledrivers Union and his long association with Local 2375 in Wilmington. He went on to explain the sign-up process and monthly dues requirement.

Being a real skilled trade, they required new members to qualify through an apprenticeship program that started at half-pay for third period apprentices. It scaled up until you passed your first period and reached full-pay at Journeyman level several years later. I had no idea there was so much involved and started feeling a little worried where this conversation was headed.

Bob said, "I've got good news for you. By graduating from that school, you qualify immediately as a Journeyman with full privileges. Not only that, you'll be paid $1 an hour over foreman's wages for all work other than diving. When you do have the opportunity to work underwater, the pay increases to $50 an hour with overtime and extraordinary circumstances negotiated to pay a premium on top of that due to hazard pay and other considerations. What do ya think? Ready to sign up?"

"Darn right!" I said, feeling relieved and stopping just short of counting the pay before I started. No wonder Al had been so insistent.

I signed up, paid the enrollment fee and dues, and was handed a brand-new Union Book and working card. Bob said we had a few more things to talk about and asked me to stick around. He had to make a quick call, but he'd be right back. Sitting back in the lobby, I stared at my new book and working card and had a feeling wash over me that I made the right decision.

Bob returned after a few minutes and said, "I just got off the phone with my contact at Alaska Constructors. They are asking us to put together a good-sized team to work on an offshore project on the backside of Santa Cruise Island. So, fill me in. What can you do out there for us? How are your burning and welding skills?"

Oh boy, I could feel my stomach begin to churn after looking at all those photos on the wall and thinking how my skills were nowhere near what I was seeing. I answered, "I'm a pretty good burner and decent rigger." Careful not to overstate my experience.

He said, "Great! I need people right away. Can you start now?"

"Now?" I asked.

"Yes. We'll be putting together crews to go offshore and cut loose the base section for an offshore oil platform. They want to drop it in as soon as Reagan lifts the moratorium."

"Count me in, but I thought that was still in place?" I said.

"Not for long," Bob replied. "Sun Oil has a platform about to show up on the backside of Santa Cruz Island where those sons of bitches in Santa Barbara can't see it. The barges and cranes are already out there and just waiting for the steel to arrive from Japan. We'll get the section prepped and ready. Just as soon as they lift that damn moratorium, we'll slide around the corner in full view of the coast and drop into the Santa Barbara Channel."

Reagan was still Governor of California at the time. It all made sense. Clearly the fix was in.

"I've been asked for burners, so we'll issue a work order for you as a burner/welder. Kathy will type that up now with contacts. You will catch the first Piledrivers crew boat out of Port Hueneme as soon as they have it scheduled in the next few days," said Bob.

I hoped the shock wasn't visible on my face, but I was already calculating what seven days a week with three weeks on and one week off schedule would look like on a paycheck. Foreman's wages plus an extra buck an hour, times twelve hours a day, seven days a week, 84 hours weekly. The math was getting hard for me, especially with time and a half over forty hours and double-time for Sundays. It would be a hefty payday out there. The base hourly rate was around $17 an hour; the gross I figured would round out at a couple of grand a week. In 1979, that was pretty darn good considering there was no diving involved, at least at this point.

Al must have known something. I doubted this was a coincidence. I accepted the work order from Bob, and after a burley handshake, he gave me direction to report as a member of the new Piledrivers crew as a burner/welder and wished me luck! Off I went. Now to explain it all to Susan. Three weeks on and one week off... Jeez Louise.

First Trip: Santa Cruz Island - Sun Henry Platform

That was a tense time, as I now had my new fiancée and two kids in a motel a little north of Wilmington after just dragging them across the country from Massachusetts. We figured we were a go for staying in Southern California, at least for now.

To leave them for the offshore oil field, working three weeks, Susan would have to fend for the gang until I got back. That might not sit well. The money sounded great but working seven twelve-hour shifts from midnight to noon was no joke. Fortunately, when Susan heard the deal, she went along with it and said with that kind of pay couldn't be passed up. Not sure we had much choice...

When I got the word on the crew boat schedule, Susan and the kids drove me all the way from the cheap motel in Torrance, ninety miles or so north to Port Hueneme. Port Hueneme was on the coast of the Oxnard plains, just north of Point Magu Air Force Base. We arrived around 6:00p.m. I was to catch the crew boat outbound for the far side of Santa Cruz Island and was expected to start that night at midnight. After hugs and a long goodbye, I boarded the forty-foot crew boat and settled in.

On the way, I had plenty of time to think of my family and ask myself how the hell I got here, all the while trying to fend off creeping feelings of doubt. The seas were good sized rolling swells as we traveled to the northwest out of Port Hueneme to Santa Cruz. The motion of the crew boat made men seasick, sending them out to throw up off the back deck.

The saltier members, mostly older and well-wrinkled, cracked open cans of sardines to eat along the way knowing they'd send a few more out back. That special smell of sardines in a closed cabin space was foul, and clearly, they were getting some sort of perverse pleasure out of clearing the cabin and leaving grown men to hug the rails topside. If it wasn't the seas, the sardines would surely get 'em.

For me, I like sardines and have never been seasick a day in my life thanks to having been raised by adventurous boating parents. My parents treated us to boating trips like taking on Buzzards Bay on the way to Martha's Vineyard.

When I was well south of ten years old, I had to take the wheel of the family's twenty-foot Sea Skiff so the rest of the family could huddle in the back of the boat to keep the bow up. My father had missed a channel marker, and there we were making our way across the Lambda Shoals outside of Woods Hole toward Martha's Vineyard.

All I could see was the sky and then the bottom of the trough of the next wave until we crossed the shoals. He was probably terrified by his mistake but made a good decision to throw me up there to steer the boat. I had no fear.

The notion of those early boating times being adventurous is a profound understatement. It doesn't do justice to what I now consider a hair-raising introduction to boating. Suffice it to say we all survived, and I credit my father for the experience.

When we finally came around the backside of Santa Cruz, it was well past sunset with darkness settling in. The Sun Oil platform base sat there on a huge barge, sprays of fiery sparks streaming like the Fourth of July.

The structure, known as the jacket, was laying sideways on the barge, the likes of which I'd never seen before. Large steel pipes were welded to the jacket to stabilize the load for the long journey, just completed across the Pacific. It was those bracings that needed to be removed to make the structure ready to set, and there were a lot of them.

From a distance, the large sprays of fire from burning torches appeared to be streaming from every part of the structure. The Iron Workers Union provided the crew for the day shift, noon to midnight, and their crews were still hard at it. Ours would be midnight to noon so when we arrived there was quite a show.

My anxiety level was rising. What I'd been witnessing, my work order said, was my job. The expectation was that I'd be qualified to jump right in. I'm a fast learner but...?

Around eleven p.m., the new Piledrivers crew was standing on the Alaska Constructor barge 333, owned by Brown and Root, and getting ready to muster for work. There was a long flat top work barge tied between the 333 and launch barge, a four hundred-footer with the bottom section laying on its side. Two Piledriver foreman were standing there, one welding and the other the rigging gang foreman, preparing to address the new crew. My introduction to this scene in the middle of the night left me with a queasy feeling and fear I'd stepped way beyond my limits when I had signed up as a 'burner.'

As the crew gathered, the lead for our group said "Welcome aboard. We have a mission to get this jacket ready to deploy. We'll assemble into two groups with riggers over here with me and burners over there with Donny."

As the ranks broke out to join their groups, I looked at the burners and the riggers and decided after what I saw from that crew boat, I was a rigger. Joining the rigging crew, I hoped to slide by unnoticed. No one had asked to see my Union work order.

Lady Luck was on my side. They took a head count, and when they found that they were short one burner, they called the hall to ask for another man. Thank god for their lousy math. I just might survive this!

The schedule was demanding, working seven twelves from midnight to noon, but I was well-suited to the rigging gang and did OK through the whole experience.

Working the overnight shift left several hours of beautiful midday California sunshine to enjoy after work. From the helipad on the end of the barge, there were panoramic views of Santa Barbara and the Channel Islands. What a beautiful place to break out the deck chairs and soak up some rays before hitting the rack around four o'clock.

We needed to catch enough sleep before our eleven p.m. wake up call for breakfast and another fantastic opportunity. Before the Ironworkers came in for dinner after their shift change, we had the choice of breakfast or Ironworker dinner. So, scrambled eggs or T-bone steaks? ... We needed a ton of calories, after all, to make a twelve-hour shift. I enjoyed Ironworker dinners. Gave me a small sense of piracy and more than a few raised eyebrows from the cooks.

After a week or so, on a Sunday, the most amazing thing happened out there behind Santa Cruz Island. As I read the newspaper after our shift, there was a headline that California had just lifted the offshore moratorium. The very next day, the tugs and barges pulled anchors, and we rounded the corner entering the Santa Barbara channel. Sun Henry was now ready to be installed.

I thought about how large a fix we were in for on this one. To design, fabricate, transport and make ready to round that corner had to have been in the planning for at least several years. To pull the trigger and execute the plan, there had to be a conspiracy somewhere. Clearly, Reagan was well connected and instrumental to the plan.

Offshore, things were great other than the three weeks on one week off thing. Food was good, weather was fine, and when Daddy got to the beach, his pockets were loaded. We were making upwards of two grand a week back in 1979, living a somewhat nomadic lifestyle.

When I reached my week off, it was vacation and party time. My beat-up Chevy magically turned into a Cadillac El Dorado. I nick named it the Blue Streak, as it carried us in fine fashion to the destinations of choice on my weeks off. We had moved into a beachfront condo in Port Hueneme and hoped for the good fortunes to continue.

Times were good. Reagan was elected President in 1980 and promised to rebuild the US Military with special attention to the dilapidated naval facilities, mostly remnants from World War 2, many in California. The former Governor of California was especially favoring his home state.

Airforce One would touch down at Point Magu Air Station just south of us when he arrived in California for time off. He flew past our condo along the beachline every time he went to his Santa Barbara ranch in two identical helicopters, one would be carrying Reagan.

After finishing up the Sun Henry platform, I went on to install another offshore rig called Platform Grace, owned by Chevron. It was also in the Santa Barbara Channel and installed by Alaska Constructors.

The Hugh W. Gordon, Brown and Root Barge 264, was a much larger construction barge than the Barge 333 used for Sun Henry. It had a Clyde crane with a 3000-ton lift capacity, 365 feet of boom, and a 28-part main block.

The crew's comfort aboard the Hugh Gordon Barge was much better. It included better food, a full bakery, and a soft serve ice cream machine.

When we finished Platform Grace it was rumored to have the most drilling conductors ever at the time in US waters. Each conductor is a conduit for a drill string that when oil was discovered, would become one oil well for production purposes. Grace had dozens; the exact number escapes my memory.

I have a bunch of stories from life in the offshore building Grace. On one of my return trips to Port Hueneme, we shared the ride with a geological survey crew that had just confirmed an enormous oil reserve in deep water in the Exxon Hondo field north of our location. They estimated the volume in the billions of barrels. The big challenge was the 900-foot water depth. Wonder whether that oil still sits there like money in the bank for Exxon today.

Having made great money in offshore oilfield construction in the Santa Barbara Channel, it was now time to move on. The Union Hall called and said they had a really good job for me. A company called Zinzer Furby from San Diego was awarded a contract to rebuild the port facilities at the Navy CB Base where we lived in Port Hueneme. The project was part of the earliest rise of the NASA Space Shuttle program and was a quasi-secret military component to support a military space shuttle envisioned to operate out of Edwards Air Force Base.

The Zinzer Furby project was a massive rebuild and hardening of the existing dock to handle large barges and heavy cranes that would be needed to support the military effort and recovery of the reusable rockets of the space shuttle. It was here where I first officially started my diving career.

The project required using divers to set several hundred, eight-foot-wide, forty-foot-long, pre-cast tee beam seawall sections. Once set, each section had two pockets formed at the base for pin piling to secure the sections to the sea floor.

A diver would guide the heavy steel H beam pin pilings into each pocket. When the pile driving was completed on the pin piles, concrete was pumped to a diver filling each of the hundreds of pockets with a hose from above, sealing the pin piles in place.

The final pour to fill the void between the existing seawall and the new tee beam sea-wall panels was over a million cubic yards of concrete. The pour was nonstop, twenty-four hours a day, seven days a week, until it was complete.

I logged a bunch of hours diving on the NASA project, plus or minus five hundred. It was a terrific opportunity, and I learned a lot of trade skills building such a large concrete dock.

Dive time averaged at least seven hours a day, four hours before lunch and at least three after lunch with an hour rollup time left to clean up in an eight-hour day.

Long Beach Navy Shipyard Rebuild

When things were finished up in Port Hueneme, I was dispatched to a project at the Long Beach Naval Shipyard. A company called Accent General was the GC and had a small contract rebuilding the fender systems and installing new camel logs.

Camel logs were tree trunk sized, and up to thirty feet long. They provided protection for the new wooden pilings we were installing. Attached by chains, they floated in the water against the pier and spanned several pilings. Their purpose was to help standoff a ship when it lay alongside the wooden pilings and fender system. By distributing the load and forces against the pilings, it would extend the life of the fender systems as well as protect ships.

The scope of work was simple. Being the preliminary stages of a major rebuild to come for Long Beach Naval Shipyard, it was great just being there. Things went well and work was progressing at a good pace. Accent General, as a company, was new to marine construction. Their company was a large industrial painting and coatings corporation out of San Diego. How they made the switch to marine construction was a mystery to me. Oh well. Pays the same.

After being on site for over a month, something awful happened. I've been urged to add this story in some detail even though it's painful to fess up to being involved.

Day of the Dolphin

The repair projects of the fender systems were spread out throughout the Naval Base. One of the finger piers, needing repair and new camel logs, had guided missile Frigates on both sides of the finger pier. Over the past three weeks, we had witnessed some activity over at that pier. It started with helicopters, swooping in with special 'hammock looking' slings and making deliveries of some sort. We couldn't see the cargo in the slings. My recollection is that there was a dozen or so of the special deliveries. Other than witnessing the drop offs, we had no idea what the Navy was up to. Didn't really care; it was none of our business.

It was my responsibility to scope out the upcoming finger pier location and determine if there were any special issues before starting the repair. I took a flatbed truck over to the finger pier, along with an apprentice, to plan for the work. When we arrived, we were missing a long tape measure needed to lay out the camel log locations in preparation of pre-staging the materials. As annoying as it was, it wasn't that big of a deal to send the apprentice back to our staging area to grab the tape measure while I checked out the finger pier and any obstructions.

About ten minutes after he left to make the half mile trip to retrieve the tape measure, I heard a loud crash. When I looked toward the end of the finger pier, I could see the flatbed stopped with the boom of the onboard mini crane swung around to the right against a Connex box located at the shoreside end of the pier. A Connex box is a special type of shipping container that can be used for a variety of applications. What was going on at the foot of the pier was anybody's guess, especially at a Naval Shipyard.

I was six hundred feet down the pier from our truck when I heard the crash and ran the distance to find out what was going on. When I got there, my apprentice was being cursed out by some Navy guy.

"What's going on here?" I demanded with a raised voice, approaching the Navy guy.

He glared at me and responded in an equally angry and raised voice, "Who the hell are you, and what are you doing out here?"

Before I could answer, a Jeep pulled up with another Navy guy. This time, it was an officer with scrambled eggs on his hat and a driver. His face was twisted in a knot. Judging by his color, he was enraged, clearly caused by whatever we'd done. In the meantime, I was surprised to see several Navy divers. They had made their way up from the water to within earshot.

"What the hell is going on here?" the officer demanded angrily, glaring at the Navy guy that was cursing out my apprentice.

"Well, sir. This flatbed truck, operated by the contractor over there, swung around the corner onto the finger pier. An unsecured boom on his truck swung free and impacted the cable array at the back of the command center. We are assessing the situation now, but it looks bad, sir."

The Officer turned to me and asked, "Are you in charge here?"

"I am." I replied.

"Please explain to me what you're doing here and how this happened.?" he asked, glaring at me. Some of the crimson color on his face was beginning to retreat.

"We're here working on the base, rebuilding the fender systems. This finger pier is on our list to repair. I had my apprentice drop me off to begin my inspection when we discovered our special measuring tool was not in the truck. I sent him back to our equipment trailer to get it. It appears that the boom on the truck crane had a mechanical failure. When he returned and made a left turn onto the finger pier, the boom swung around to the right and impacted your trailer," I explained, maintaining as much professional calm as possible under the circumstances. I hoped to answer his questions and make the case that we were authorized to be there.

He looked back at the other Navy guy and asked, "Why weren't these guys stopped and this reported?"

"I'm sorry, sir. We were preoccupied with operations and divers in the water with the dolphins. We didn't notice, sir, and had no orders to post guards," he replied.

"That's unacceptable," he said as he turned back to me. "Do you have any idea what you've done here?" he said seething with anger, "You've destroyed over two years of work! Every one of those cables was custom made. There are no spares. It'll take another year or more to repair all the damage." With that he turned, glared back at that other Navy guy without saying another word, and got back into his jeep. His driver sped off toward an administrative building off in the distance.

After he left, I asked my apprentice to pull the boom back into position and properly secure it. There was no need for further discussion, especially with that other Navy guy standing there. When we backed out to leave, I could see another group of divers still in the water with dolphins hanging at their side. It was then that I fully realized how much trouble we were in.

We returned to our construction trailer, fully expecting to find a crowd of Navy people ripping into our Superintendent. When we pulled up, the only truck there belong to Dale, our guy. "What was going on?" I wondered to myself as we entered the trailer.

"Hello there, Dale. Did you hear anything from the Navy about our presence at the finger pier?" I asked.

"No. Should I?" he asked looking at the apprentice.

I asked my guy to step outside so I could talk to Dale. "Well, we had an incident."

"What? What kind of incident?" asked Dale.

"We scoped out the finger pier over there where the Frigates are tied up and needed a long tape measure to lay it out for access and materials. I sent our apprentice back to the trailer to get it while I started to look around. When he came back, the boom on the truck crane swung around to the right when he made the turn and slammed into the back of the Navy Connex box. It hit squarely on a massive cable array. Looked like it wrecked a bunch of the cables," I said.

"Oh my God!" Dale said as he fell back into his chair.

"There is something else you should know," I continued.

"There's more?" Dale asked with panic beginning to show on his face.

"Unfortunately. The Navy was conducting some sort of 'special ops' training with Navy divers and dolphins. I didn't quite know what to make of it until some guy with scrambled eggs on his hat showed up. Not sure I've ever seen anybody that angry before. From the color in his face, I thought he was having a stroke."

Dale just sat there staring at me.

"I was surprised to see they weren't swarming the place when we got back," I said.

"What's next?" Dale asked, looking up from his desk.

"I don't know, but I'd wait for them to contact us before doing anything. Can't see any upside to being proactive or reaching out to them before hearing something. We'll find out soon enough." *Great advice,* I thought, given how far my ass was hanging out.

"OK," he said, "but stay away from there until we figure this out."

"Fine by me. We have plenty to do."

"Let's have a conversation about this later. We just got a bid package in for another big project out here. We'll need to huddle up on the new bid once the dust settles. That is, if they don't throw us out!"

"Agreed. I'm going to take the apprentice back over to the tool trailer and tell him to keep his mouth shut," I said as I turned to go out the door.

"Should we let him go?" asked Dale.

"Don't think so, but I'll let you know how our conversation goes," I said.

"Fair enough. Let me know as soon as you can. We need the help." With that, we had to get back to work. Only time would tell what was coming our way. We'd just have to wait.

The next day, I saw the helicopters return with their special lifting hammocks, remove the dozen or more dolphins, and fly off to the south. I waited a couple of days and sent spies for a drive by to see what was going on over there. Amazingly, they reported back that the Connex box was gone and there was nothing left behind, other than the two Frigates. Like it never happened ...

That was really strange. What were they doing over there?

What a mess. Dale said the Navy made no mention of the incident. It must have been a black ops project we stumbled across and wiped out. There is no other explanation for why nobody showed up from the Navy following our disaster. We were left to continue our project. Thank God.

Time to move forward and look at the new bid package. We were confident in successfully completing the existing project. If we had a shot to hang in there for a major rebuild, it would be great.

Bid Request – Structural Upgrade – Full Pier Plus

Accent General had an opportunity to bid for a much larger contract to rebuild a long, robust-looking pier. The pier number escapes my memory but was a major pier, fifteen hundred feet long, with room for several ships to dock. It may have been large enough for aircraft carriers.

The scope of work was large and included replacing most of the existing pilings with new hundred-foot pre-cast pilings. Hundreds of holes would be cut through the existing deck to set and drive the new pilings. New pile caps would be formed and installed under the existing deck on top of the new pilings to support and reinforce the pier.

There were many bidders, but the biggest head scratch of the bid request was the demolition of a massive boat ramp that was inset at the end of the pier. The bid required removal of all the old pilings and deck leaving the adjacent pier and deck intact.

It would be a tough challenge to remove without damaging the existing pilings and deck on each side of the ramp. It was such a huge task that every bidder would have a considerable number in the bid for this item.

A pal of mine and I had a great idea, and we got with Dale, the Accent General Superintendent to lay it out for him. The idea was to saw cut the ramp completely free from the existing pier. One of our welders had a plan to add on to ours. He proposed to fabricate a four thousand pound, pointed demo tool, that we could dead drop from a crane and break the concrete decking.

That would expose all the underlying pilings from the section that we would cut free from the pier, above and below the waterline. The exposed piling could then be easily removed with the deck gone. By using a high-pressure water jet attached to a long pipe, the old pilings could be loosened and pulled out with a crane. Once we had all the pilings removed, we'd use the crane and a clam bucket to remove all the remaining concrete. Genius! We thought.

The secret to our proposal was to use a large hydraulic wall saw to cut each side of the ramp underwater from the bottom in about fifteen feet of water up to the waterline at the top. Each saw cut would be around a hundred feet in length underwater. The saw could continue from the water and in the dry until the ramp was cut free from the rest of the pier.

It would require a lot of diving to complete, if we got the job. The big hope was that with the larger scope of work, there would be plenty more to do underwater.

Dale said, "What the hell. If you guys can make that happen, we can throw a number at it and just might have a chance." He called his office and filled them in. The bid was due by the end of the day.

In a couple of days, we got a call from Dale, "We got It!" he said excitedly. Fantastic news for us and a great project with a lot of side benefits. In a couple of months, we tooled up and moved in to begin the project. It was a blast! The full scope of work had a ton of important things to build and terrific plan, all thanks to our bid-winning boat ramp demo idea.

When we finally got to the demo of the ramp, everything went as planned. We saw cut the ramp and jetted out the piling with a huge bonus. The pier had been there for decades and had also been closed for a long time before we tackled the project.

When we jetted out each of the pilings, they were loaded, top to bottom, with the largest rock scallops I've ever seen! In the shell, they were the size of dinner plates. The meat from each scallop weighed between a quarter and half a pound and were as fresh as any I've ever tasted.

The scallops were in high demand. We made lots of friends on the Navy base, including the officers with scrambled eggs on their hats like the one we were terrified of earlier with the dolphin fiasco. They showed up every afternoon around four o'clock and helped themselves to the scallops that we heaped in a pile at the end of the pier. Week after week, we did this daily for them and the rest of the crew to grab...

The losing contractors all wanted to come by and see how we did this. Hey, fine with us. No secrets here, just imagination! We were elated.

For me, the project added another bunch of dive time, at least another 300 hours, plus all the scallops you could eat!

California Dreaming - Yokohama Fender System

After wrapping up the work at the Long Beach Naval Shipyard, I got a call to work on a special project. It was the installation of the first Yokohama Fender System in the Western Hemisphere for large ships in commercial ports. JH Pomeroy from Petaluma, CA had been awarded the contract and would be my new employer for the project. Pomeroy was a large outfit with international credits. They had just finished a large Navy project building a huge base somewhere in the Middle East. Sounded good to me.

The Yokohama ship fender system was the first of its kind to be installed in the Western Hemisphere. It was a collection of large rubber drums with ten-foot by ten-foot square Teflon plates on their faces for ships to lay against in port. They had potential to replace the traditional wooden piling fender systems common since the beginning of time on the waterfront. Those had required frequent and costly repair. The new system, if successful, could be great for the expanding Port of Long Beach. The Union Hall Business Agent, Bob, knew this was a big deal and pulled me in to help.

I had a good reputation for getting things done, and the Yokohama system could be a lot of work in a place as large as the Ports of LA and Long Beach.

Working down in the port, we had a favorite restaurant and bar called Pegasus, where we stumbled into every morning at 6:00a.m. We ate breakfast and headed to the job site not more than half a mile away. We rallied there again late in the afternoons for a couple of cold ones before heading home. Their claim to fame was fine food, ice cold beers, and service by highly attractive, scantily clad waitresses. Didn't matter what time of day: breakfast, lunch or beer-thirty in our case.

Turns out the Yokohama system was not that complicated other than having to adapt to the existing conditions in the port. It was an excellent job on the waterfront in the Port of Long Beach. It was working there that I met an interesting guy at Pegasus, Don Risk. Don was an accomplished retired Navy diver. He had gone on to a career in the commercial diving industry following retirement from the Navy and worked as President of Taylor Diving Services. They had over a thousand divers on the payroll and worldwide operations.

Don had burned out due to the stress of running such a large organization and somehow landed as a regular at Pegasus. He was not only a giant in the commercial diving industry, but as a Navy diver, had been a crew member on SEA-LAB II.

SEA-LAB II was a joint effort between the Navy and NASA Astronauts. It was a grueling 45-day project where three teams of ten Navy divers spent 15 days each in an underwater habitat placed on an undersea canyon ledge off

La Jolla, California. Mercury 7 astronaut, Scott Carpenter, spent the first thirty days leading the teams. Carpenter and his team members swam down the 200 feet to the Sea-Lab II habitat on August 28, 1965. The first group took up residence, starting the event.

Don's stories were awesome. Sad part was meeting Don after he crashed and burned, hanging around Pegasus drowning his sorrows. We found him there every afternoon after we wrapped up for the day down in the port. Hmm, could have been worse, thinking about those waitresses. I made sure I got Don's contact info.

We successfully finished up the Yokohama Fender System, and there was talk about JH Pomeroy moving the whole operation to Florida to build the new Sunshine Skyway Bridge. Our gang didn't make the trip due to Florida adopting the 'right to work state' position. Being Union, it wasn't going to happen. The going hourly rate for 'right to work' labor was around eight bucks an hour, less than half what we were being paid for topside construction.

JL Meeks - LA Harbor - Huntington Beach Pier

Work was starting to slow down in early 1984, and the dispatches for new work opportunities were drying up. I went by the Union Hall to see what was going on and get a feel for where things were headed. When I was there, Virgil Hollins, another Business Agent at local 2375, came out to see me and said he just got a call from JL Meeks. At the time, JL Meeks Construction had been around LA Harbor for decades. They were small but very well respected around the Ports of LA and Long Beach. Meeks was looking for someone, and Virgil thought I could be a good fit. It might lead to something good or at least a bridge to a better opportunity. I accepted the call.

I worked on several special harbor construction jobs for Meeks. Most of their projects were anywhere from a day to a week or two, but once again, my luck would help me out. They bid on the demolition of Huntington Beach Pier. It had been severely damaged. The end of the pier collapsed during the great winter storm of 1983. Meeks was awarded the demolition with the rebuild contract to be bid out sometime in 1984. They were in a rush to get the demo done and clear the way for the re-construction ahead.

There was a fair amount of diving work involved with the project and Meeks wanted me to do the work. One problem, I needed a tender and didn't have one. I remembered Don Risk and wondered if I could talk him into signing up to help at Huntington Beach? It wouldn't be a strenuous job for a tender. Even at his age, I had no doubt he was more than capable.

I stopped by Pegasus after work looking for Don. Ah ha, he was there. "Hey there Don. What's going on?" I asked.

"The usual. I think I'm in love with Heather," he said.

"She's too young for you, Don."

"I can dream. Order me another beer," he bellowed.

"Hey, I need a little help. The new outfit I'm working for bagged the contract to do the demo on the Huntington Beach Pier, and I got the job doing the diving piece."

"Great news!" said Don, on his way to three sheets to the wind.

"I've got a big problem though, I need a tender," I said.

"Well that sucks. What are you going to do?" asked Don.

"That's why I'm here talking to you. How'd you like to spend a few weeks making a good paycheck and hanging around Huntington Beach?" I asked.

"Are you serious?" he laughed.

"Sure am. It would be a blast! Hey, you might fall in love again down there! Quite a show around the Pier. They don't have binoculars up and down on the Pier for nothing. Besides, it's honest work, and I can help get you signed up with the Union. It's up to me who Meeks hires as my tender. What do you think?" I prodded.

"I don't know. Well, it beats doing nothing but waiting to come down here every day. I'll do it," Don said, shaking his head.

Time enough for one more beer. We shook hands, and I told him I'd call the Union Hall to let JL Meeks know he was going to be my tender.

What an unbelievable thing. I think of Don Risk as a bit of a national hero, being a SEA-LAB II crew guy and Naval Commander. The whole Taylor Diving thing was great but not the true measure of the man. It was a humbling experience and great luck at the same time to have him working with me at Huntington Beach. Technically he was my tender, but seriously? I was honored to have him onboard.

Don showed up at Huntington Beach on our first day out, and sure enough, the sites were spectacular. He had brought his scrapbook and had a great custom-made silver hardhat from Taylor Diving. What a collection of photographs. His best photos were from inside the oval office in dress whites, receiving awards from President Lyndon Johnson. He and Scott Carpenter became great lifelong friends. Amazing.

At Huntington Beach we had a meeting on site with the City and walked the end of the Pier with our crane operator and the restaurant owner, John Gustafson. John was the owner of 'The End Café' which had been destroyed in the storm. The City and Gustafson were extremely helpful and gave us a way of determining when we reached our depth at the bottom of the debris pile. The end of the Pier had been taken out by the storms in the past, and they said to be on the lookout for black and white checkered tile, bathroom flooring from decades before and considered the bottom layer.

The pier was a major attraction and centerpiece for Huntington Beach. When we moved in and started to survey the debris field, a photographer from the local newspaper took my picture hanging off a chair being lowered by our crane operator, Woody. Great picture. I used to have a copy, but I guess it's still in a newspaper archive somewhere.

What a mess. Broken deck sections and debris everywhere. If I could break the sections into small enough pieces, Woody could lift them out of there. How do you crack a slab in twenty feet of water? Believe it or not, we rigged up a ninety-pound jack hammer on the crane and lowered it to where I could break the slab sections and rig them for Woody to pull. I fabricated an airlift to remove large volumes of sand and clear a way to get a sling around the concrete pieces of decking. That was painful but an effective way to get rid of the large obstructions and decking. The sound of a ninety-pound jackhammer underwater was excruciating.

The excavation went on for more than two weeks before finding a small piece of flooring with black and white tiles. We'd reached the final layer, a small corner piece about 18 inches across. We showed it to Gustafson, and he quickly offered to buy it from us for display in the new 'End Café.' We gladly gave it to him, free of charge.

It was great having Don there. He carried a large pile of dimes with him every day to feed the binoculars during our lunch hour. I used plenty myself dripping water all over the deck from my wetsuit that I didn't bother to take off for a half hour lunch break. What a great job. I logged another 150 more hours of dive time over the course of the project. Unfortunately, I would not be around for the rebuild and re-opening in 1985.

California to New England – Time for a Change

Following completion of the demo at Huntington Beach, my time was over with JL Meeks. Their work had slowed to a point that they were forced to lay everybody off except a couple of guys that had been there for decades. Back at the Union Hall, there was nothing but hopes for the work to pick up. Can't pay the bills with hope.

In the end, not all good things last forever and this being no exception, the bottom was beginning to fall out under Reagan. The economy was in trouble and scaling back on military and oilfield expenses was the result. Work slowed and eventually reached a critical point. Huntington Beach Pier would be my last job in California at that time.

With work in marine construction and the offshore oilfield slowing dramatically in Southern California, it was time to figure out how we'd survive. The income needed to provide for a young family was growing. With reliance on being dispatched as needed for work from Piledrivers Union 2375 now spotty and even more of a challenge, we had to make a change. Susan and I now had four children and were forced to pull up stakes and head back to New England to reach for a fresh start. I hoped to find the breathing room needed to shift gears and land us back on our feet. We made the decision to go, with the only question being when. Kids school and other things had to be weighed before pulling the plug.

We packed up the family not long after my Huntington Beach job and headed east. We arrived back in the Boston area and stayed with Susan's parents, Charlie and Dory Proctor, in Ipswich for a while. I had to come up with a job. My skills in both marine construction and commercial diving were strong, but I was willing to do whatever was needed to survive and move forward. Times were beginning to get desperate. Without Susan's families support, we would have been in real trouble.

CHAPTER FIVE

BOSTON RESTART

Boston, the HUB, as the locals call it. That would be short for 'Hub of the Universe.' It was comforting being back in familiar surroundings but challenging not knowing what people were doing to survive the economic downturn.

My oldest brother, Jay, a Suffolk Law School graduate and accountant, was similarly in need of a break. He struggled with the bar early on after Law school and worked as an accountant for years in the firm of one of his best friends, David Keefe.

He was also hoping to do better for his family, especially as his daughters would be approaching college age before too long. We got together out at the lake in Brimfield where Jay lived. After he made us a couple of extra-tall Rum and Cokes with a couple of lime wedges, we sat on lounge chairs on the large deck off the back of his house overlooking the lake.

With the sun shining through the pines and a soft breeze blowing, it was a beautiful thing. I filled him in on our situation and my need to come up with a job to kick-start our life back in New England. We talked about the good old days when he lived on the Danvers River. We laughed about all the small boats and outboard engines he bought and my paddle wheel canoe I put so much effort into in '76.

I couldn't help but remind him about the special phone call I had with his wife Julie years ago, when he was out on the river in one of those small aluminum boats he collected.

Jay was having a tough time starting the outboard motor on a boat he just bought. He was pulling the starter cord over and over when it finally fired up; the boat took off down the river leaving Jay tumbling out of the back into the water. He had forgotten to take the motor out of gear before pulling the starter rope.

I was on the phone with Julie and got a play by play of what Jay was doing on the boat, when she suddenly exclaimed, "Oh my God. Jay just fell out of the boat! The boat's taking off down the river! Oh no, it's starting to turn. I've got to go... I think it's going to run him over!" Click, as she hung up the phone.

I jumped in the car and rushed the five miles over there to find out what was going on. The boat did in fact make a wild turn and attempt to run him over. Jay said he was able to deflect the bow and suck in his gut as the propeller whizzed by. The boat circled again and again, tighter and tighter, until finally spinning straight up in the air and dropping engine-first back in the river. We spent the afternoon that day doing salvage.

We laughed like hell remembering the day and Julie's panic! We had endless stories of small boating adventures, but this one was special.

Finally, after a long visit and a bunch of laughs, Jay suggested I go see our old family friend George Osgood. George was Jay's best friend since childhood and owned a small steel erecting company, Marblehead Steel. He put up industrial buildings around Massachusetts and New Hampshire and stayed very busy.

When I was a late teenager, I had worked for George before I knew anything about construction. Jay called him, and he agreed to rehire me.

George was a hard-driving and self-made man, proud of all he had accomplished and rightfully so. He made his bones by having been a welder and foreman building the World Trade Center buildings in New York. I started back to work for George as a crew lead of sorts and enjoyed the simple pleasure of steel erecting. Especially after the gigantic nature of offshore and marine construction in California, it was a relief and a soft landing.

All was going well for six months or so, other than the constant calling I felt to return to the waterfront. One day the phone rang, and it was Charlie Wilkerson.

Charlie was a child of privilege. His father was an accomplished diplomat who served as Under Secretary of State following WW ll. He was well educated, a colorful man, and an author. With his service in the Navy Submarine field, he had penned stories including one on the impact that mini subs had in World War II with the Japanese, Italians, and Germans. He would eventually give me an autographed copy of that book. A great read.

As for Charlie, he had been living in DC with his parents and sister for years before finally moving back to the family estate, a large mansion overlooking a rocky point in Swampscott, Massachusetts after his father retired. It was at that estate where he awaited his inheritance and worked hard at trying to look worthy of the family fortunes.

I had reached out to Charlie when I got back from California, at the suggestion of my brother Greg. He had bumped into Charlie somewhere along the way. Greg said Charlie was starting a diving business working on ships. When I called him, he wasn't very receptive to me. He felt that his new company, Sub Scrub Specialists, with his brother-in-law running the operations, was well on the way to success. They had hired a handful of scuba divers to run the machinery and were just waiting for the jobs to come in. With some limited advertising, they were able to capture a job or two.

Charlie's eventual call, I would learn, had come only after their failure to complete a simple scope of work and handle their new machinery on a small Greek tanker. The pathetic performance in the real world, with everybody on the ship looking over the side, was no way to start out. He decided to track me down and have another conversation.

"How's it going?" Charlie started.

I was caught off guard by the call and the tone in his voice. I knew something was up. I said, "I'm doing well. How's your hull cleaning business doing?"

"Well, not that great. We had a couple of jobs and had equipment problems," he said.

"Equipment?" I asked, knowing all the time they were doomed from the start after our first conversation.

"Yeah. The hydraulic brush machine didn't function properly, and we couldn't maintain operational control with a man riding the machine as designed. It had too much negative buoyancy and immediately sank to the bottom. There was no way a man could drag it off the bottom and get it back to the ship hull to make it work."

No kidding, I thought, especially in Scuba gear, once again remembering our previous conversation when I blew off the idea of working with him. He told me they spent over a hundred grand on the hull cleaning equipment, and none of it was working properly.

There was a pregnant pause before I asked the obvious, "So, what can I do for you?" I felt bad for him, sort of, as I had tried to head this off in the past conversation.

Charlie said, "How about coming over to hit a few balls and talk about things. Early next week?"

That would be tennis balls on the clay court next to the Carriage house that Charlie lived in at the mansion on the bluffs in Swampscott. Well, that was a head scratcher. Maybe there was an opportunity here after all. Certainly, worth whacking a few tennis balls to find out. Charlie was a big lefty hitter with a killer serve. He may be better on the tennis court than I but not so much as a commercial diver.

We had watched all the ships heading up and down the channel while hanging at Pegasus in the Port of Long Beach. No future in working on ships that we could figure. From what we heard, it was a dud, lousy pay, and unpredictable. Maybe, with one exception, I thought. As an owner operator, maybe the pay wouldn't be that bad. Could make this a viable option. If played right, might even evolve into something special. I agreed to meet Charlie and hit a few.

We met and played for a while before going out for lunch and drinks. I listened at length to the sorry tale of 'Sub Scrub Specialists' and the final humiliation that caused Charlie to re-consider his options. Charlie's lead diver was a childhood neighbor of mine from Marblehead neck, Harry. I guess that was not too surprising. Harry grew up on the harbor front in Marblehead and was comfortable in and under the waters around greater Salem Bay.

Charlie pitched me on the idea of coming onboard to help pull things together. He was sure we could make this work and offered a partnership position. The pay sounded short but doable. After all, it made sense to make a sacrifice to buy in on a startup.

We parted company with me agreeing to think it over and get back to him. With a family, looking at a new start up, there was a big risk. Steel erecting was not likely to make me enough money in the long run to move forward with a young family, so I called Charlie and agreed with caveats. The first being that 'Sub Scrub Specialists' had to go. Charlie agreed, and with that, I made the commitment to jump in.

The Company

Having scrapped Sub Scrub Specialists (SSS) and its hideous logo, it was time to invent the new brand. I reached out to another one of my brothers who was a marketing guy, Dana. He had worked for years in marketing and sales for large corporations and traveled extensively for business. I felt he had a good sense of what would be needed to start the process.

First thing was the new name for the company. We brainstormed to come up with a suitable name and high-level business concept. After kicking it around, he came up with Aqua as a start. Begins with A and implies water. Pretty good, I thought. Needed an ending, Facts, leading to the question what facts? Not exactly knowing where this was headed, he suggested an off spelling of facts to fax, like the new technology at the time. I didn't like the name ending in 'X.'

After a little back and forth, we came up with Facs. Sounds a little like a drunken slur but when put together it looked surprisingly good: Aquafacs. Different. The new name was coined with logos and branding to follow. I brought all this back to Charlie and pitched the name. He bought in. Probably just to keep me onboard with this insanity.

Things were starting to take shape. We now needed to find people with qualifications and willingness to buy into the new Aquafacs dream. That's truly all we had to offer, a dream. My oldest brother Jay, both a lawyer and accountant and living with his family out on the lake in Brimfield, would be a great place to start. He had taken a shot at running a convenience store out in the small town of Brimfield and was forced to give that up due to lack of income stream. It was also difficult to keep up with the petty theft, common with convenience stores. After a lengthy conversation, I asked him if he was willing to take another gamble with Aquafacs. Who knew where it might lead? He accepted.

It turns out Charlie had a family lawyer, Bernie something or other, likely Charlie's father's attorney. Part of Charlie's requirement to move forward was the understanding that his family lawyer would assist with the incorporating of Aquafacs and necessary filing to get the new company papered.

Charlie, with some family money in play, would lead the company as President. He had no concept of commercial diving but was well heeled and presented himself well. I would be acting VP and function on operational and engineering issues. Jay would come on as Treasurer and function with accounting tasks and financial planning. So, there we were, the principle partners of the new Aquafacs.

We needed to spin up an office with laydown and storage space for us to start from. Charlie had some luck finding an office for rent on the waterfront in East Boston. We met at Pier One in East Boston to check it out. What a great sounding address if this worked out, Aquafacs, Pier One, East Boston. Even better, our neighbors would be the Boston Harbor Pilots, lending legitimacy and maybe opportunity with our presence on the waterfront.

We met the agent for the Port Authority to get in for a look at the office. It was one large room and took up the northeast corner of the building on the first floor. The office had a bathroom and a full line of windows on both the north and east walls making for good natural lighting and working environment.

Not a very fancy office but the location and address were amazing. The next thing we'd need to check out was storage space. The building itself was a large open warehouse with tall roll up doors on all sides. There was a channel on both sides, and it opened to Boston Harbor to the south. We asked the agent if we could use the warehouse for storage. He said it was available as a small add-on to the rent. There were other businesses that we saw already operating inside the building.

Other than the rollup doors, there was no climate control in the warehouse. It would be a cold place in the winter. We'd have to work out the details later if we leased the location. We agreed this would be the new home for Aquafacs and requested our lease include about fifteen hundred square feet of floor space out back. The agent agreed to write it up. Done deal.

Charlie had stored all the Sub Scrub Specialist equipment at his family's estate in Swampscott. Time to round it up and bring it to Pier One. The office setup would be easy, as it was a first-floor location. We still had one more hurdle, security out back. The bare floor space was handy, but without enclosed storage, it would be impossible to protect the diving equipment we'd be using. Jay came up with a simple and affordable solution, renting a portable storage container. We pulled the trigger and rented a forty-foot container on wheels where we could lock up valuables and provide a workshop space for repair. Problem solved.

Now was time to inventory what equipment Charlie had left over from the Sub Scrub Specialists debacle and determine if anything was commercially useable going forward. We had to be prepared to field diving crews and perform whatever and wherever we were lucky enough to come up with. It was disappointing to find that SSS had no useable equipment except for a couple of scuba tanks and standard regulators possibly useful as safety equipment. When I joined Charlie in this adventure, I made it clear that we were not going to use scuba ever for commercial work. Safety issues like lack of reliable comms to and from the diver and working around ports with tugboats and large ships made scuba unacceptable, full stop. We had little to build on other than a dream and dogged determination.

We spent hours in our new office going back and forth on how to move forward. What were we doing here? What could we realistically offer for services? How do we access the shipping community and develop connections? So many questions. Equipment could always be acquired, but the number one thing we needed was sales. No work, no company. Simple as that.

CHAPTER SIX

LUCK OF THE IRISH

The one thing we did know was that New York was the center of the universe for shipping, Manhattan specifically. Battery Park and Mid-Town were filled with shipping companies and operators.

At the time, there was no internet or easy way to figure out how to gain business. My brother Jay had an 'old school' idea, shoe leather. He'd cold call on shipping companies where they lived in lower and midtown Manhattan.

He persuaded us that for short money, he'd catch the Amtrak Banker train from Springfield to Grand Central Station and hit the bricks. Simple plan, enter a Manhattan high rise office building, check the marquee, and cold call anyone with Shipping or Maritime in their name. He'd size them up, and if they owned or operated ships, he'd pitch 'em on Aquafacs.

His pitch would be to offer hull and propeller cleaning and inspection services. Never mind that we had no workable equipment and little more than anecdotal knowledge of hull cleaning from the failed experience of Sub Scrub Specialists.

We were a long way from being ready to operate. It was absurd, looking at the pile of junk we had out back at our newly leased office with a prestigious sounding location, Pier One, East Boston.

Off he went. Jay started his adventures, pounding the pavement in Manhattan. And so, it was on one day in late April 1984, while I was working on an equipment plan just in case, the phone rang. It was Jay calling from New York.

"Hello there, Chris. I'm here with my new friend Keith Duncan. We've been talking about all the services Aquafacs has, and he has something we might be able to help him with. Keith works for Maritime Overseas and wants to know if we can put divers inside Supertanker cargo tanks to perform survey work. He has two Supertankers in the Canary Islands and wants to know if we can help and would be interested in working with him?"

I nearly dropped the phone. There was only one answer, as insane as it was. "Sure, we can. See what he needs to move forward, and we'll be happy to help him out."

"Thanks Chris. I'll call you later to discuss details." Click went the phone as Jay hung up.

I almost fell out of my chair. What the hell is a Supertanker?

We would come to learn that Supertankers were also known as VLCCs (very large crude carriers.) Typically, the Supertankers of the eighties carried six million barrels or more of crude oil and were so large you virtually never saw them. They were unable to navigate coastal waters due to their deep draft, in excess of seventy feet. Along with carrying six million barrels of crude, they were behemoths, often a quarter mile long, three hundred feet wide, and with hundred-foot deep tanks. They were designed to carry large volumes of crude oil from places like the Middle East, North Sea and Alaska to refineries or lightering points where they would offload. Smaller tankers would complete the carriage to the refineries in the East, West and Gulf coasts, along with St Lucia, St. Croix, and a few other ports in the Caribbean.

The industry decided to adopt a new set of inspection protocols. The new rules were drafted to offset the concern for the safety of Supertankers and the possibility of catastrophic oil spills in the case of structural failure and loss at sea. There was just cause, as the ships were single hull vessels and fractures were being found in the gigantic ships during drydocking cycles. This was years before the public uproar over the fouling and destruction of the pristine Alaskan coastline by the Exxon Valdez in March of 1989. The rules were being drafted by IACS (The International Association of Classification Societies.)

For Aquafacs, this was no joke. A real fire drill with real ships in the Canary Islands. Not only that, we would learn that Maritime Overseas was the single largest carrier of crude oil on the planet at the time. Leave it to Jay to catch the whale.

In Tank Inspections, Maritime Overseas-Work Scope

Back in Boston, when Jay arrived, we had a good laugh!

I asked, "What the hell did you do? We don't even know what a supertanker is, not to mention that we have no equipment or know what kind of equipment we'll need. Now what? And what's that IACS thing?" Didn't matter we were going to make this happen...

Before parting, Keith Duncan provided Jay with a copy of the proposed new rules, along with names and contacts at both Lloyds Register of Shipping and American Bureau of Shipping (ABS,) the two largest Classification Societies at the time.

The American Bureau of Shipping, the second Classification Society we would need to work with, was founded in 1862 with operations mirroring Lloyd's. It would be a valuable resource, located in Manhattan. They had information and the publications from their view of the new upcoming rules. There were several other Classification Societies that were party to the proposed changes, but for our purposes, Lloyds Register and ABS were our focus as the two ships in the Canary Islands had one of each Class...

The International Association of Classification Societies, IACS, would be required to execute and enforce any changes that might be adopted by their new rules. Not very popular within the shipping community, to say the least.

Now we had to figure out what the scope of work would entail. What did Maritime Overseas need from us to perform this experimental underwater trial? How would they comply by offering the use of commercial diving as part of a larger methodology if the new rules were adopted? We would have to figure it out. We had the new rules and a high-level view of what would be required, and that was all.

It was becoming clear that our new friend Keith Duncan had something more in mind and was trying to find the right crew to work with. I guessed anonymity must have been key, because certainly nobody had ever heard of Aquafacs. And if we failed, it would be Aqua who?

The new rules were specific, calling out requirements on a sliding scale based on the age of the ship. Everything was straight forward, except it was all contemplated to be done in the dry. What the Keith Duncan method was proposing was to comply by using divers and doing all the work underwater. The new rules required ultrasonic thickness gaging of the steel inside the tanks along with visual inspection for obvious cracks in already known suspect areas. Not that big of a deal until you consider the quarter mile length of a Supertanker. How exactly were they going to do this?

We learned that the typical Supertanker in cross section view was three tanks across. Starboard wing, center tank (largest of the three,) and port wing, with the three tanks collectively forming a girth belt. That designation was critical to the new proposed requirements. The first inspection cycle would require compliance on two girth belts. Bottom line was that six tanks would be inspected with ultrasonic thickness testing and visual inspection requirements. Doesn't sound that odious until you consider the size, configuration and construction of the ships. The typical center tank was two-hundred-feet long, one-hundred-feet-wide and one hundred-feet-deep with gigantic ring webs of steel forming the structural components of the internals.

To access the crude oil cargo tanks inside a supertanker there is usually only one way. You need to enter through a hatch and climb down a hundred-foot rung ladder all the way to the bottom of the tank. There were rarely step off points or inspection levels. The only way to get a good look at the inside of a tank and gage any steel in the dry would require pipe staging. It would be lowered one piece at a time to the bottom of the tank and assembled as a nearly hundred-foot-tall tower to reach the underdeck.

When they completed inspecting a location, they would have to disassemble the entire staging tower and move over to the next location to reassemble as they worked their way across the tank collecting data and close visual inspection, per the rules.

Much of their concerns were the under-deck plating and structural steel in the upper regions of the tanks. All the ship's structural steel is inside the tanks so the crude oil sloshing around was a major corrosion concern. As they plied the seas from source to refinery, rusting or cracking was considered a rising risk factor as the ships aged.

If a single-hulled supertanker rusted through the one-inch thick shell plating, a major oil spill could occur. Or if the corrosion of the under-deck caused an area of thinning of the deck plating, it could pose a personnel safety issue. If a man stepped on a weakened section of deck, it might fail, causing a man to fall through into a tank, likely a deadly accident.

Supertankers posed an awesome challenge. The new rules would be a showstopper, nearly impossible to implement and the cost would be astronomical. For Keith Duncan and Maritime Overseas, as the world's largest oil carrier, it could be a large financial handicap and interfere with their operations.

His experiment in the Canary Islands with Aquafacs was a Hail Mary. If he succeeded, he could push back on the rules, and worst case, he'd have invented a process that just might work to mitigate the cost and time required to survive the new rules. The stakes were huge.

As for us, we were completely oblivious to the big picture ramifications and highly charged politics of the proposed IACS rules change. Good thing for us, as we were free to tackle this at face value and stick to figuring out how to pull all the pieces together, literally. Duncan assigned two trusted Marine Engineers to support our efforts, Joe March and Dick Spoor. Their help was invaluable in schooling us up in a hurry about all things Supertanker. They would accompany us all the way through the project and attend in the Canary Islands.

Reality Check and Engineering Marvel

Back in the real world at Pier One, we had absolutely no diving equipment. No helmets, no radio comms, no stills cameras, no umbilicals, no lighting, no plan for prolonged compressed air, no suits, simply nothing at all... with two Supertankers on the book.

There was a company in California that specialized in commercial diving equipment, Amron International. They were an outfit I knew about from my days out west. They were acting distributors for all things commercial diving and when it comes to equipment, kind of like Grainger's for commercial diving gear. Time to go shopping.

I had to figure out what our diving equipment needs would be to work inside of a huge oil tanker. For starters, we needed two top of the line diving helmets, at a minimum. Kirby Morgan Superlight 17B was a great choice. We bought two with simple spare parts kits.

Two diver communications radios were added. They could be used singly or stacked for multiple users so topside control could hear and manage both divers if two were in together and could be tied in directly to the overall system for data recording purposes. We didn't expect to need that often, as all the tasks were typically a one man show. It would also build in redundancy should we have a radio fail in the Canary Islands.

We strung together two, three-hundred-foot air umbilicals with comm lines. A whole compliment of ancillary equipment and a compact high-pressure compressor to fill tanks that would be racked to a manifold for air supply was included.

Incredibly, we had no time to test anything. UPS came every day in early August 1984, and the contents were checked and then loaded immediately into crates and prepared for shipping. We would be packed and ready. Just one thing missing. Crew!

So, we had no crew, and we'd need world-class divers that were fast learners and great actors. Somehow made me think of the Paul Newman classic, The Sting. As I contemplated how we could pull this off, I considered myself a capable diver, so there was one for the crew.

I gave Mudshark Mulroy a call. He was unable to join the crew but said, "Hey, call Stevie. He works with a bunch of guys that are all totally World Class."

I called Steve and filled him in on what we were cookin'.

He laughed his ass off, "You gotta be kidding?"

"Nope," I said, "this is what we got. What do you think?"

He said, "Let me make a couple of calls and get back to you. How many guys you need?"

I told him, "I think we need at least three divers plus me to make this happen."

"OK. I'll call you back," he said.

An hour later, he called, "I've got two so far, me and my pal Mark Duffy. We're working on a third guy, either Billy ('Basketball') Jones or Eddie Phillips, great guy with a terrific sense of humor. I'll round up one of them."

"Great! We can use all the humor we can find with this one," I joked.

Stevie asked, "They'll all want to know what's up, how long, how much we're paying and how we're going to play this?"

"Answer is, not sure, probably a couple of weeks plus or minus, pay negotiable but good, you can help me with figuring that, expenses paid and whatever it takes to play this and succeed..."

Holy smoke, I thought. *Play this? Yeah, sure.*

He called back and said "Mark and Eddie Phillips are in. Plus, me. I wasn't doing much right now anyway. Would have liked Basketball, but he couldn't break free from some high-altitude dam project that was paying way too much to give up for a trip to the Canaries. We can discuss pay and the rest when we pull this together. We got a deal?"

"Great news, you bet!" I said. He had no idea how relieved I was that we now had a team that just might be able to make this happen.

We left it that we would arrange for all to arrive in Boston two days ahead of the flight to the Canary Islands, leaving time to go over everything and develop a plan and strategy. Surely guys from Lloyds and The American Bureau of Shipping, not to mention the Reps from Maritime Overseas, would have plenty of questions about us. Like who we were and where the heck did we come from?

With all the diving equipment finally in house and a plan for the highly specialized diving crew, we now had to complete our technical package.

We were incredibly lucky as we found we had a lot of friends close by who were interested in what we were up to. MIT was just down the Charles River. They had all the talent we'd need. We had a special contact with a family connection to the former Sub Scrub Specialists. The guy was the uncle of Harry Noyes, former scuba diver for SSS. Peter Noyes was an expert in fiber optics and would pair that with the ultrasonic testing system and signals to remotely test the steel thickness inside the tanks.

We were hoping to provide the data onsite by way of using a diver to locate and test areas within the tank while providing video documentation of the live time progress.

Our goal was to feed the audio/video and the ultrasonic gauging data links remotely to a large video monitor and record everything on VHS tape. Turns out Peter and friends were able to accomplish what we needed by combining all the technology. The final product would be a VHS tape of the survey with time and date stamp, along with a simultaneous video display of the thickness gauging in real time.

By recording the divers hand applying the ultrasonic probe to a marked location with the diver audio recorded, there was never any doubt about where we were. All the testing and visual observations would be made for the inspectors to observe. They would all stay topside and view the action on the color monitor we brought with us.

With good two-way communications between the diver in the tank and topside team, the inspectors would be able to ask questions and help direct the actions as we proceeded. Points of interest could be explored to their satisfaction.

This was all 'Star Wars' stuff at the time, fed by fiber optics. The whole system was tested and functioned in the dry, but it was yet to be tested in saltwater. Mere bench testing was all we were going to get before heading to the Canaries. Peter Noyes would join the crew for the Canary Island projects just in case...

When the dive team finally huddled up in Boston, I had a fun time laying this out and watching their faces. Stevie Richards, Mark Duffy and Eddie Phillips clearly had never been a part of anything like this before. With international backgrounds and years of experience, they were all in and ready to play Aquafacs employees. Highly competent in ultrasonic testing and any other darn thing we needed, well that was our story. The crew was set. All would play along and keep our Aquafacs team a tightly held secret...

We had no idea what we'd stepped in or how deep, but it was clear we were all the way in. Some of our planning required meetings with the Maritime Overseas Marine Engineering Department. Joe March and Dick Spoor would attend for Maritime Overseas to help with logistics and anything else they could do. They knew all about how the game was played and would handle the ABS and Lloyds guys once we got started. Charlie and I met with the head of The American Bureau of Shipping, Ken Amer, prior to departure. He had requested a meeting to go over our plan. They were going to attend the first of the two ships, and he wanted to make sure we were ready.

I'll never forget that meeting with Ken. His parting comment was, "I don't know who you guys are or how you got into this, but I just want you to know, if you so much as fart in the Canary Islands, the smell will reach here long before you return." Wow, that was encouraging.

Lloyds was located down in Battery Park, and they didn't seem to have much interest beyond a meet and greet. Their guys were coming from Europe somewhere to attend the trials in the Canaries. They'd hear about it later. Cordial enough. Brits.

CHAPTER SEVEN

THE CANARY ISLAND SUPERTANKERS

On August 18th, 1984, our crew boarded a flight from Logan to Madrid and connected to Gran Canaria on Iberia Airlines. The two supertankers lay rafted together alongside a sea wall at Las Palmas. Fitted with docking hardware and a finger pier to access the vessels, we would have no problem boarding both ships.

We had a six-man crew in total working for Aquafacs in Las Palmas. Few details were spared in looking the part, down to Aquafacs tee shirts and full white coveralls with names and logos like NASA. If that wasn't enough, we had branded ball caps to protect from the searing sun in Las Palmas. For insurance, we were glad to have our MIT pal Peter Noyes along. All the electronics had to work. If anything went wrong over there, we hoped to God he could troubleshoot it and fix the problem. This was 1984 after all.

Joe March and Dick Spoor met us at the hotel in Las Palmas where we introduced them to our crew. They quickly became our best friends, tour guides, and were as helpful as possible. The Aquafacs diving crew, except for me, had all worked together in the past so there was a natural chemistry and incredible sense of humor within the gang. You would never know they had just come together to play Aquafacs. We knew Joe and Dick had a huge personal stake here and were determined to help us succeed for Keith Duncan and the cause. Game on.

When we showed up at the first tanker, we found that all of our equipment had made it and was on the deck waiting for us. There was nothing but brand spanking new everything. We looked great! I wondered if Joe thought about how great.

Maritime Overseas clearly must have paid for this fine equipment. Ah, no more than a drop in the bucket compared with what they were undertaking. Fine by me. Once we did our thing and succeeded, we'd make it back to Pier One and might actually have equipment we could use to be a real diving company. A win-win...

Showtime.

We mustered early on day one of what we expected to take two weeks to complete, one week per supertanker starting with the American Bureau of Shipping vessel. Joe March brought us aboard to meet the layup Captain, have breakfast, and then begin the set up to get everything underway.

The Captain was an elderly Italian man who spoke perfect English. He seemed incredibly friendly and happy to have visitors other than the Korean crew that helped maintain the two supertankers in layup. He had no cooks that could make anything remotely Italian, though they were constantly willing to try. We knew he was in trouble when we saw what they thought Americans ate for breakfast. They thought we preferred a bottle of Heineken beer to a cup of coffee as a drink with the meal. Every meal came with a Heineken. The Captain apologized.

After breakfast, we spent an hour or so briefing the Captain with Joe March and filling him in on what we were doing for the next couple of weeks. We agreed to start each day with breakfast onboard with the Captain and only asked that he somehow figure out how to replace the Heineken with coffee... He succeeded.

Screwing everything together and setting the stage for the upcoming trials took a while as everything was new, and some assembly required was the joke of the day. In the end, we had provided and shipped absolutely everything we needed, and the crew worked like a military drill team to prepare the dive station and technical gear on the deck near the first tank we would enter. Once we had power properly available at our command location, our MIT guy, Peter, decided to join in as a member of the crew and started putting the technical equipment package together. We were a well-oiled diving machine, at least in appearance. Joe March and Dick Spoor looked encouraged. If they only knew.

The diving equipment and ancillary materials were assembled by the dive team without hesitation. Tested and placed online, we were ready to dive. Our HP compressor whirred quietly, filling the cylinders we'd bank together for the breathing air supply. Hardly needed to utter a word. It was all moving forward like any other day on the waterfront.

Our video system, ultrasonic testing equipment and tie into the diving station was being wired up and tested by Peter Noyes with the help of Charlie. They seemed to work well together which helped take some of the pressure off and kept Charlie busy.

We now had to concentrate on what we were up against. How to enter the tanks? What lighting would be needed? What hazards might be found inside the tanks? How would the visibility be for video and stills? What safety protocols might be needed? And so on until we were comfortable and ready to deploy.

Once we had the dive station online at the first center tank, I dressed in and entered the tank. Climbing through an ullage opening (a raised, oval shaped hatch,) it was easy to access. The sea water was filled to the top of the tank, a few feet below the rim of the hatch. It was a simple climb down a few rungs, and I was in. I dropped down twenty feet or so and checked the water clarity and overall visibility. It was awesome! Nearly gin clear.

There were small overhead ports along the deck, above on both sides of the tank running fore and aft. They were for something called COW guns (crude oil wash system.) The light streamed through like skylights, revealing an eerie crystal-clear bluish water and showing off the tank internals and structure.

Our entry point was at the back end of the tank. Looking forward, there were gigantic steel ring webs visible. One after another, after another, on and on until reaching the bulkhead two hundred feet forward. Clear visibility all the way to the forward end of the two-hundred-foot long tank left me no doubt there would be terrific opportunity to capture what we came for.

I clicked a couple of photos of the amazing view looking forward, and then I exited the tank to meet with the crew and go over the plan. Joe came by to ask how things looked. I could hardly contain myself while telling him we were looking good and ready to start.

The ABS Reps were due to arrive the following day, and we arranged to be ready and start the work around noon. We would have a short briefing and then start the show. I would stay topside and lead the survey with the help of Dick

Spoor of MOC. Joe would hang back with the ABS guy and Charlie while we moved forward with our plan.

    We based our day-to-day operations on meeting the minimum requirements for the new IACS rules and limited our work to the upper half of the tanks at depths not to exceed fifty feet, unless there were points of interest either MOC or the ABS Rep wanted to view or test. The theory was that when the tanks were dry, the lower half would be easily accessible for inspection and testing. This would help lengthen the amount of daily dive time for our inspection and testing. Made sense.

    Amazingly, all of our equipment, diving and technical, came to life and worked flawlessly the entire time we were in the Canaries. The ABS guys were wowed by the video quality, and our recorded ultrasonic thickness data was something they'd never seen before in this kind of setting or any other to date. It's likely this was a world's first. They knew this was special, and when we completed the requirements and walked through all their concerns, they left. We had no doubt that smell Ken Amer had warned us about had turned into roses. Joe March and Dick Spoor were so relieved at how well things had gone, they said we're going to take a couple days off and go down to Maspolomis on the south end of Gran Canaria for a little R&R. We were all going along as well.

    When we got there, we found out that the place was a favorite European get away, a clothing optional kind of beach. The further from the hotel you got, the less clothing or none at all. Turns out the area was developed by the Germans, and there was a fine beer garden every couple of hundred yards, all the way down the beach. With fine sights, fine food and strong sense of how well we were doing, we all enjoyed the short break. We knew we had this one in the bag.

The reps from Lloyds were coming for the second ship trial. So, after two days off, we traveled back to Las Palmas and shifted our gear over to the second supertanker. There was no reason to think there would be any substantial difference between the two supertankers, and our Italian Captain was Master of both. The routine would continue. Breakfast aboard and then on to work.

It was almost surreal. My lead guy in the tank would do the beginning introduction to the new Lloyds start up. He started his narration with, "This is Mark Duffy reporting from inside a supertanker, currently sitting in lay up in the Canary Islands."

I stepped in and asked him to begin with the proper ID we used for setting the stage each day as we worked through the surveys. I had to think he was feeling the same confidence we all were, that this was a done deal. Aquafacs had pulled it off. We just needed clean professional video and commentary only.

Success

We finished up with the Lloyds classed vessel without any issues, and our Lloyds Rep went on his way satisfied we'd completed our task. We were left with Joe and Dick Spoor impressed with our performance and more than a little relieved. Before we broke down the dive station on the Lloyds vessel, Joe asked me if he and Dick could have a crack at using our gear to get a look inside. They virtually had never seen the underdeck areas of any of their ships, and the chance to swim around and look at all these things they've been seeing and hearing on our video was something they may never again have an opportunity to experience. How could I say no?

I asked Eddie to dress in and be their tour guide. It was such a pleasure getting Joe dressed in wearing one of our shiny new Superlight 17s and helping him into the tank. Eddie held on to his harness and led him around the upper sections of the tank to his delight. We had their comms linked so they could talk to each other, and Eddie was a pro, leading Joe where he wanted to go. Dick would follow second and was treated to the same Eddie Phillips show, complete with wise cracks and bad jokes.

The following day, Joe March and Dick Spoor would head back to New York, while we packed up our gear and made ready to depart. Our crew left the next day, but Charlie and I stayed an extra day to decompress and enjoy the glow of success. I wondered if Charlie ever really believed we could pull this off. I had no doubt we would, especially after that first look inside.

This may have been the successful end of the operation but only the beginning of the follow up. That would include preparing a close out report and God knows where things would go from there. Keith Duncan had never asked us how much this would cost. I had to think, now that we'd succeeded, he was on the hook. Guess he might now have what he needed, succeeded for his purposes, and proved himself as Master of the Game in tanker world. We'd learn later that no one was surprised. He was in fact a legend in the industry.

CHAPTER EIGHT

SOCIETY OF NAVAL ARCHITECTS AND MARINE ENGINEERS – AQUAFACS PRESENTS

After completing the close out documents and forwarding on to Joe March, we received a call from Keith Duncan inviting us to New York for a sit down to discuss upcoming events. It turns out there was a group in the maritime community that assembles annually and hosts the latest people and topics of the time. It's called the Society of Naval Architects and Marine Engineers. (SNAME.) Turns out that 'In Tank Inspections' was the hottest topic of the day with the looming IACS rules change. Exxon was the headliner, having spent a fortune working with a company to develop a program very similar to what we'd accomplished with Maritime Overseas.

What do you know? Taylor Diving. Don Risk's old company. They were the largest and most respected commercial diving company at the time and had been contracted to use remotely operated vehicles (ROVs) to conduct internal visual inspections of Exxon supertankers. Exxon felt their work was groundbreaking and relevant to help solve the challenges of inspecting the internal structures of supertankers.

So, there it was. Keith Duncan, leading the largest fleet of crude oil tankers and supertanker fleet, had quietly undercut Exxon with the Aquafacs work in the Canaries. He was ready for Exxon and his push back against the IACS rules. Keith asked that we select a couple dozen photos in slide form and be prepared to provide a follow-on presentation to show how Maritime Overseas generally agreed with Exxon's efforts. His story, how MOC had developed a process to perform a proper steel inspection that could meet the requirements of the upcoming IACS recommendations should they be adopted. Seemed reasonable enough.

He arranged with Exxon to allow us an opportunity for a follow-up with a few photos loaded up on the backside of their slide show. We would be able to speak on Duncan's behalf about our work in the Canaries, following the Exxon presentation. He said he'd be there to support our effort. Oh, boy.

The Presentation

The special presentation for 1985 at the annual SNAME gathering was being made by Exxon. They were considered the leaders in driving new methods of inspecting the structural integrity of supertankers in advance of the IACS rules under development and close to adoption. They had utilized new robotic technology to perform the inspection in the tanks filled with ballast water and pressed up to the top for ease of operation. Sounded familiar.

We knew they were teamed up with Taylor Diving, but we had no idea what they had accomplished and would have to wait for the presentation to see. With our experience in the Canaries, we had observed and had to contend with steel scaffold brackets welded all over the interior of the tanks. We were forced to untangle hoses and other cables frequently as we moved ahead with our work. It was a simple task by our diver in the tank and performed mostly without any interruption to the program or noticed by those watching topside.

Exxon had several dozen slides to go along with a narrative on how they had performed their trial inspection. The slides were fairly good, and the direction they were headed sounded positive. When they summarized their results and plans to further develop the methodology using robotics, it suddenly became clear this was a work in progress and not a proven method like we had recently completed with MOC in Las Palmas.

Keith had made the connection for us with Exxon to provide a supporting follow-up to their program. We placed the dozen or so slides at the back of their tray prior to the show and arranged to be recognized when they had completed their presentation and brief Q&A. They finished to a polite applause from the crowd.

Their speaker then introduced Charles Wilkerson with Aquafacs, speaking on behalf of MOC. "Aquafacs, working with MOC, will provide a brief further discussion in support of our presentation," he said.

As Charlie headed to the podium at the front of the exhibition hall, a booming voice from the back of the room loudly filled the hall. All heads turned; it was Keith Duncan.

Leaning against a column, Duncan proclaimed, "I can shed some light on this. Maritime Overseas has undertaken a plan that employs a similar methodology as our friends at Exxon, but realizing the physical limitations of being able to successfully access the internals of the tanks, it would require more of a hands-on approach. We have performed a trial on two of our VLCC vessels in lay up in the Canary Islands. Using well-trained steel inspectors in diving gear with the latest available technology, we worked toward the same end as what you've just witnessed from Exxon. They have been good enough to allow us to show a bit of what we have done to promote our concept of 'In Tank' inspections. We put this forward tonight as a viable plan to comply with the requirements of the upcoming rules, should they be adopted by the community. I would like to introduce Charles Wilkerson with Aquafacs of Boston to show where we've been in this development. Charles?"

The crowd turned back to the front. Charlie was ready to deliver. He pulled up the first slide, and there were audible gasps as the crowd viewed the stunning view and clarity. The subject was the long view of the ring webs in the center tank I had photographed that first day.

Charlie droned on, slide after slide, narrating all the while how we had moved from tank to tank, collected the data, and recorded the findings. We showed a great photo pulled from the color video showing the hand of the diver with the ultrasonic probe applied to a steel bulkhead. The data box on our CCTV screen showing the readout at the top.

There was nothing like that in the Exxon show, only promises to continue the development. We were showing the real deal. When we reached the end of the slides, Charlie wrapped up the Aquafacs narrative in smooth fashion and thanked Exxon as well as the crowd. There was enthusiastic applause for our mini presentation. I was thrilled and felt we did well for Duncan and his pursuits.

Little did I know how well we did. The crowd flowed out into a large hallway outside the presentation venue, and it was there that we found Keith Duncan and the VP of Exxon Marine going at it. The VP from Exxon was really pissed and claiming foul.

He loudly dressed down Duncan for having upstaged the finely tuned presentation by Exxon. "How dare you come here and show all those slides without clearing that with me first? I would never have allowed that. We have invested highly in this program and plan to move forward with perfecting the protocol."

Duncan said, "We've already proved the ability to conduct the protocol and furthermore ran the trials with ABS and Lloyds in attendance. Our data was spot on, and you could see the quality of the work and technology we developed."

They went back and forth for a good five minutes. Duncan finally suggested that Exxon go back and figure out how to match their progress. To paraphrase, he said something to the effect of "put your money where your mouth is or piss off," as only a well-schooled Brit can say it.

Duncan turned away and wrapped his arms around Charlie's and my shoulders and said, "Let's go boys." And off we went, out to a bar not far from the venue.

Keith bought us all a round and proposed a toast, "Well done gentlemen! To Aquafacs." We all drank. The bar was the legendary Fraunces Tavern, established in 1762 in New York, going all the way back to when it was still a British Colony. Seemed somehow fitting with Keith Duncan, another Brit, leading the way.

He had bested Exxon. Listening to them at the event, they seemed full of themselves, and clearly Duncan had taken them down a notch and humiliated their VP in a most public kind of way. I was concerned about having participated in such a public flogging, especially after learning how small the maritime community was.

So, there we were. Now the newly famous masked men from Boston. Nobody knew who we were, but we had lit a fire and everyone in the industry had smelled the smoke. We now had to figure how to take this incredible luck and parlay it into the business. The reality is that we did a spectacular job pulling this off, but we were still left with serious problems, like no crew and only a small pile of good equipment. None of which was for cleaning ships or anything previously contemplated as 'ships husbandry' capable services.

Stevie, Mark and Eddie returned to their world class diving pursuits, and we were left to figure out where to come up with qualified diving personnel and how to move on from here.

CHAPTER NINE

REALITY SETS IN

Incredibly, we not only had the great luck with Jay having knocked on Keith Duncan's door, but our SNAME appearance had introduced us to the highest echelons of the Maritime Community. Not surprisingly, our phone began to ring with calls from agents and interested ship owners who wanted to know more about Aquafacs. We didn't exactly have four color brochures we could send them, or anything else for that matter. What we did have was only our recent fame and a pile of brand-new diving gear. We'd captured the interest and imagination of an otherwise stuffy business.

I was in the office continuing the organizational task of shaking out what we now owned for equipment and trying to determine what capability we had, if any, should Aquafacs get a real call for service. Sure enough, the phone rang. The incoming call was from a guy with SOHIO (Standard Oil of Ohio.) "Hello. This is Robert Smith with Sohio Marine. Who am I speaking with?" he said.

"Good morning, Mr. Smith. You have Charles Wilkerson and Chris Lee here. How are you sir?" we asked.

"Well, very well indeed. Thank you. Call me Robert." He went on, "I was at the SNAME presentation and was fascinated by how you were able to develop the technology and the results that your slides showed. They left no doubt that you fellows were far ahead of where Exxon was in their efforts. You'll forgive me if I say, we at SOHIO really enjoyed the show."

I'll bet they did, knowing how we had inadvertently humiliated Exxon in front of the entire global Maritime Community. Robert Smith was VP of the Marine Department at Standard Oil and claimed he was extremely interested in our in-tank inspection solutions. Having been at the SNAME meeting, we had little doubt he was genuinely sincere. In hindsight, he was probably more interested by our relationship with Keith Duncan and how he had outmaneuvered Exxon. Why not get it from the horse's mouth, Aquafacs being the horse.

Robert continued, "That Duncan fellow with Maritime Overseas is a cagey old fox. He really did a wonderful job of adding to the Exxon discussion." Feigning clearing his throat, "Well, actually more like showing Exxon how this could be done properly." Robert seemed to be enjoying our conversation way too much. He went on, "I'd like to come by and meet you gentlemen in Boston. Would you mind if I stopped by? Say later this week?"

Well, that was fast. We were more than happy to hear what he had to say and see if there was anything we could do for SOHIO. "Sure Robert. We'd love to meet you, and Wednesday or Thursday look good."

"I'd prefer Wednesday if that's OK. I'll be coming alone."

"Sure thing," we said, "How about a lunch meeting? Boston has a great reputation for sea food."

He chuckled, "No, but thanks. I won't be able to stay that long." What kind of an answer was that?

My ears perked up. "OK Robert. We'll look forward to seeing you. Before or after lunch? Your call."

"After," he said, "around one o'clock should work. I'll call you when I arrive and catch a cab from Logan. Have a good afternoon gentleman. See you Wednesday." Click. The phone went dead.

What the hell was that? After researching who this guy was, we got another shocker. We had the top Marine Engineer at SOHIO in the Marine Group coming to Boston to meet us. This had to be more than a meet and greet. And what was that 'I'll be coming alone thing' and not being around long enough for lunch or anything else? Guess we'd have to wait and find out. His office was in Cleveland, and I started to wonder if he might have been on his way to New York via a quick side stop in Boston. But why?

He arrived on Wednesday and called as scheduled. Thirty minutes later, the cab showed up at Pier One. We were close to Logan Airport on the north side of the tunnel.

Robert Smith, we now knew, was an older and well-educated gentleman with decades of experience, another giant in the Maritime Industry. He was well-respected, and everyone in the business knew him.

We met Robert at the front door of Pier 1, and after a short exchange of pleasantries, he said he was getting ready to retire. He looked old enough to have retired years ago... We invited him in and offered him a chair and a drink of his choice. At the time, alcohol was still on the menu of choices, and we had plenty of it. Mostly for medicinal purposes rather than social at this point. He chose water.

We had a friendly conversation about the structural issues with supertankers and the changing rules. He asked probing questions about Maritime Overseas and how they'd come to work with us in the Canary Islands. I had a strong suspicion he knew more about that then we might imagine. SOHIO had the same exposure as the rest of the industry, and if IACS went forward, it was a global issue.

The meeting went on for over an hour discussing our new process. I'm sure he was sizing us up, and after looking around at our office, confirmed his suspicion that Duncan had ginned up this whole thing including Aquafacs, no more than a local Boston outfit that he used to drive his experiment with little risk and potential for high reward if it succeeded. And if not, no one would ever know.

Robert didn't seem that interested in what we had to offer SOHIO for other services or maintenance, but he leaned forward and said, "I have come across something we are extremely interested in. Have you ever heard of propeller polishing?"

"No," I responded, "we have equipment to clean propellers of marine growth but never heard of propeller polishing." The honest truth was that we knew nothing about propellers at this point.

Robert continued, "I just met a young man from 3M, Robin Pitman. They have developed new abrasives and a way to not only clean large diameter propellers but polish them leaving a virtual mirror finish. We at SOHIO are very interested in this, and you just might be able to pick up on this and give us more to talk about going forward. As a matter of fact, I think they are an hour or so behind us. So, if you'd like, I'd be happy to call Robin and see if he's around."

"Sure thing," I said to Robert, not realizing just how important that call would become in the life of Aquafacs.

He picked up the phone and dialed. We hit the speaker phone button, "Hello. Is this Robin?"

"Yes, it is."

"Hello there. This is Robert from SOHIO. We just spoke the other day."

"Hey there, Robert. Good to hear from you. What's going on?" "

"Well, I'm here in Boston meeting with some gentleman that recently showed up in New York at the SNAME conference with an interesting presentation on tanker inspections. We talked, and I told them that we were really interested in what you were doing with polishing propellers. I'd like to introduce you to Charles Wilkerson and Chris Lee with Aquafacs."

"Great! Hello gentleman. My name is Robin Pitman with 3M, Special Projects Division," he said. "What did Robert tell you?"

"Nice to meet you, Robin. We had a nice chat with Robert, and he kept turning the conversation back to propeller polishing." Robert Smith grinned. "We heard you guys had something special. He said if we could figure this out, we might have something good to talk about, and SOHIO would be very interested."

"Sure, sounds like a great opportunity," Robin said. "I heard you guys were in Boston. Any chance I can come by and fill you in? There's way too much to discuss over the phone."

"Sure thing," I said.

"I can be there in the morning around ten," said Robin, "Would that work?"

"Tomorrow? We'll be here. Pier One, East Boston. Easy to find. Call when you get in town. See you tomorrow," I said as we wrapped up the call.

Robert said he had to leave and asked us to call him a cab. We offered to run him back to Logan, but he declined and thanked us for taking the time to meet with him on such short notice. He must have only planned to stop in Boston just long enough to blow by our office and hit the trail either home to Cleveland or off to New York. He didn't say which, and we didn't ask.

When his cab arrived, he thanked us again for our time, especially with the short notice, and asked us to get back to him after we met with Robin Pitman. As for the in-tank thing, who knew? No sales there, yet. Probably never even in play, only us.

Propeller Polishing

Robin Pitman showed up at Pier One at ten in the morning as scheduled on the following day. We had no idea what to expect, but considering where we were as Aquafacs, this could be a big deal.

Robin, it seems, was a great guy with a big problem. He was a commercial diver, but not only that, an incredibly special type of commercial diver. He was a hyperbaric welder performing deep-water, high-pressure pipe welding in the offshore oilfield. For the uninitiated, that's about as difficult and demanding a skilled trade as anything on the planet. It is also incredibly dangerous and was in high demand as the oil industry marched forward to develop more and more crude oil. At increasingly deeper and more difficult locations offshore, the need for innovation was critical to save time and increase safety.

    Robin was looking for a solution to a very specific problem. He had great difficulty with removing an extra-tough epoxy coating applied to steel pipes beneath an overcoating of concrete, used to add weight to hold the pipeline in place on the sea floor. When preparing to tap into an existing pipeline, all the concrete overcoating had to be removed to expose the existing pipe wall. The thick layer of epoxy coating had to be completely removed to allow for the welding of a new pipe section. Completing a tie in was tough enough battling the harsh conditions on the sea floor without having a second battle with the epoxy.

    This was a critical issue. The amount of time needed to demo the concrete weight coating off an existing pipeline and somehow scrape or grind the epoxy coating off the steel pipe so they could make a hot tap took way too long. It was exhausting and added another layer of risk. The cost and wear and tear on equipment, combined with the added stress on the commercial diving welding teams, made Robins mission not only a critical need but potentially lifesaving. The underwater pipelines he worked on were located everywhere oil rigs needed to pipe their crude oil ashore or other pipelines transiting long distances for supply delivery. He needed help.

    Robin contacted 3M, masters of the abrasive materials world, and ran his problem past their engineering department. They were interested, or maybe sympathetic. Not only did they agree to work with Robin but in fact hired him. They built special testing tanks and pipeline mockups in Minnesota, and Robin led the development effort to come up with an abrasive solution that he could take back to the deepwater oilfields. Genius, I thought.

Robin worked together at 3M and developed eight-inch diameter donut shaped discs made from what they called Scotch Brite material. The discs were made of nylon and carbon fiber impregnated with silicon crystals with a density and shape that when spinning at high revolution, could remove the stubborn epoxy coating with ease. They were hollow in the center so that when spinning in water created a strong suction allowing for good control and relative stability. They were attached to an aluminum hub by way of a special Velcro that would allow a diver to quickly change out a disc if needed and continue his work. Fantastic discovery and invention.

Not sure what people know about 3M, but some of their most successful products came about from great ideas gone bad. Think post-it notes. Long story there, ultimately successful. In this case, what they developed worked to perfection but for... Ah the but. Do the math. How many hot taps are going on out there in the world, and what are the sales projections for the new product for 3M. The answer, few and not much. Robin was left, as many inventors, in need of something to juice up sales or product viability to at least keep things going. 3M was working this as a special project, but at some point, it would have to prove its value to the business or be cut loose.

I listened intently as Robin went on and on with the history of his work and involvement with 3M. Seemed like he was getting close to the end of his story when he said, "You're not going to believe this. When I tested the latest density and grit of the eight-inch discs in the tank, I noticed how much better these worked and how shiny the steel had become after removing the epoxy layer. In fact, I could see my face on the surface of the pipe. Later when I was back in the office and trying to think of how else or who else could benefit for these discs, it donned on me that if the disc could do that to a steel pipe, what could it do to a large bronze ship propeller? I had some experience inspecting ships along the way and was always amazed at the size of those things." The ultimate ah-ha moment.

Robin went on to say that he arranged a test on a large ship propeller in the port nearby to test his theory. After a few minutes of spinning that eight-inch 3M disc, he was looking at his face on the propeller blade. What a moment. He finally might have what he needed to not only keep his pet project moving but give 3M enough potential for sales that they might allow the program to move forward as a product. These might actually make it.

3M loved the idea that Robin had a viable prospect for another groundbreaking product. They were thinking way ahead. Think military and naval applications. Aircraft carrier propellers, nuke subs, and so on. Maybe even an international market. For Robin, he would undertake the role of marketing and sales. They gave him a big title, and he was on his way, sort of.

He would be responsible for sales and approaching the shipping industry, proving to them the benefits and fuel savings they could see with regular cleaning and polishing the propellers on their ships. Early estimates were that the savings could be as high as three to five percent per year in fuel cost.

So here we sat listening to his incredible tale, and it was clear to me that for him to show up like a lightning bolt after that call from SOHIO, there was a missing link.

Robin Pitman was a pipe welder with no real connection to the shipping industry other than a bit of cold-calling sales where he met a few operators, including our new friend from SOHIO. What he did not know, and we were quickly finding out, ship owners hated divers. Every time they hired divers for anything, it always cost a fortune with mixed results. At the very least, the reports from the field were unreliable and left a bad impression, especially at upper management level in the maritime community. They all had horror stories and after all, they couldn't see what was going on down below and had to rely on the report from a diver they did not know or trust. The one thing they did know was that there was a big bill coming every time they called for diving services.

The biggest challenge for 3M and Robin Pitman was how to establish credibility with the shipping community. Not so much for them as the need to somehow rehabilitate the image of 'the diver' and how the new process was going to be implemented. No small feat there and no wonder he showed up at Pier One. We were a company with newly acquired credibility, having just arrived on the scene and presenting at SNAME. We just might have broken through that trust barrier with ship operators and become the fresh start needed by a service company to bridge the credibility gap. We had enormous potential to make propeller polishing and maintenance using the 3M system a reality. The head of the SOHIO tanker division clearly recognized the opportunity for Robin and connected the dots to Pier One, Boston, and Aquafacs.

CHAPTER TEN

SPIN OF THE WHEEL

We were excited about the opportunity, but for no equipment, no knowledge nor any expertise with large diameter propellers, we had a long row to hoe. All we really knew was that there were a lot of ships out there, and we had better be fast learners. Robin Pitman's comments helped begin a dialog the see what Aquafacs could do for him and 3M. We needed more information and a quick education on propellers. So many pieces and moving parts. Robin answered our basic questions and assured us that we would have the full backing of 3M if we made a commitment to help run with this.

He said, "If you guys tool up, we'll support you at 3M and provide all of your materials for as long as it takes to prove propeller polishing works to the Maritime Industry. For smart ship-operators, this should be easily embraced. It would lower their fuel costs, the single largest operating expense. Should be easy to sell."

And without having to say it, he was surely also thinking of selling a bunch of polishing discs. The opportunity was enormous. There was only one answer; we were in.

Following our SNAME debut, we had been contacted by an agent who provided services and support to the Shipping Industry. His name was Richard O'Boyle. We agreed to meet and go over what Dick was saying about how he could help Aquafacs access the industry and develop business opportunities. He claimed to be well-connected and capable of aiding in our business development by representing us to the industry and his client base.

He was a rep for several highly skilled service companies that specialized in maintenance and repair of steam and large diesel-powered ships. Helping us figure out how the industry worked at the maintenance and repair level was what we needed for opportunity to move forward. After our meeting with Robin Pitman, it was time to reach out to Dick and see what (or who) he knew about large diameter propellers.

We spent some time explaining to our new agent how we had just come to find out about propeller polishing and our new friends at SOHIO and 3M. He had never heard of the process but was keenly interested and knew just who else would be. Sure, everyone with a ship, I was thinking.

Dick, however, really knew all these guys and we didn't. He was a Kings Point graduate, the most prestigious Maritime College in the country, the Harvard of Maritime colleges. How to get in front of the right people to pitch a proposal for propeller maintenance, or any other thing we could sell, would be worth the ten percent commission we agreed to. It would give us an active and motivated sales presence, a win-win we figured.

Having told 3M we're in, it was time to sink or swim, literally. We had to go to school as fast as possible on large diameter ship propellers. Dick O'Boyle must know people in the propeller industry, and that he did.

As luck would have it, the largest US manufacturer was Ferguson Propellers, located in Hoboken, NJ. He was friends with the owners and often helped them with repair and logistics when one of their propellers was damaged somewhere out worlds away from Hoboken.

He also had connections at Bird Johnson Propellers which was one of the largest manufacturers of propellers for the US Navy, including highly skewed submarine propellers and controllable pitch propellers that allow a ship to go from full ahead to full astern by merely rotating the blades of the propeller on a hydraulically operated hub. They were in Walpole, Massachusetts just down the street from Boston. Time for Dick O'Boyle to start earning that 10%...

Ferguson Propellers – The Education Begins

Turns out, Dick was not just a friend, but a very close friend, of the owners and folks at Ferguson Propellers. We sure needed to know a lot more about propellers before claiming to be experts. Propellers were incredibly expensive to buy, and that was only the first piece; then you needed to install it. That was done in a drydock somewhere. Bottom line, the last thing a ship operator wanted was a diver with a grinding tool working away on the propeller. The potential for damage was enormous.

O'Boyle arranged for us to meet the team at Ferguson and take a tour. It was unbelievable how large these things were. They had propellers thirty feet in diameter, weighing in at mind boggling numbers up to 265,000 lbs., and made of solid nickel aluminum bronze (NIBRAL.) Each propeller was stamped on the casting with the diameter, date of manufacture, and weight for each propeller. Their name, of course, was also stamped into the casting found between two of the blades on the hub of the propeller.

The facility was huge, with an equally huge laydown yard. Dozens of propellers were packaged up and ready to ship. Some of these were so large they could only be transported by barge or ship for delivery to the drydock destination. Supertanker propellers were the granddaddies of propellers, up to thirty feet in diameter and most difficult to manufacture and transport.

We met the General Manager and his staff when we entered the plant and were shown how they manufactured the giant propellers using a specialized sand-casting process.

Molten NIBRAL material was poured into the prepared sand castings and set aside to cool. When ready, they were removed from the castings and inspected for quality to confirm the correct geometry and certified weight.

Once the inspection was completed, they polished the blades and hub to a high degree of finish and then prepped them for delivery. It was an awesome thing to see and a great starting point for my education.

We had lunch with the GM and other staff members of Ferguson, where we shared our goal to pursue cleaning and polishing propellers in the field during normal operations and cargo delivery in between dry dockings. They mentioned a concern about the geometry of the propeller blades and the potential disastrous consequences if we somehow changed any of that by grinding away on a propeller underwater.

I assured them that the abrasives we were going to use were developed and tested by 3M and showed little to no risk if the process was completed properly. Not sure they were convinced by my comments. Oh well, they seemed friendly enough and wished us well, offering to be available should we need help or have any questions as we came across any of their propellers out there. We were sure we would, if this program got underway.

Standing next to those castings lying flat on the floor of their plant and seeing the finished products being readied to ship was something special and worrying at the same time. How the hell were we going to polish one of those things to a mirror finish out in the wild somewhere. To complete the work while they were in service meant traveling to meet the ship, in port or at anchor somewhere. Work would have to be completed without interfering with their scheduled discharge times in port or wherever? Guess we'd find out. We were all the way in, again thanks to Sohio.

In the meantime, we got a call from Dick. He told us he was a member of the Whitehall Club, an exclusive private club catering to the high mucky mucks of the shipping industry in NYC at the time. After mulling things over, he had an idea for something special. He had to investigate it before telling us.

He called back later and filled us in on his plan. We would host a white tablecloth luncheon with his help at the Whitehall Club. The topic: Propeller Polishing, a simple fuel savings initiative.

As a member, he said he was able to work out a deal with the club to host the luncheon. It would be by invitation only and figured it would be well-attended and a tough ticket to get, given the venue and free lunch outing.

He would require invitees to RSVP, letting us know just how serious a luncheon we would muster. Great idea!

We ended up with a full house, all hand-selected by Dick O'Boyle. He knew all the players in the industry, including both engineers and buyers.

We contacted 3M. Robin was thrilled at the idea; he agreed to attend and present to the group on behalf of 3M and their support for us. Dick also arranged for us to do a live time trial on a small tanker operated by Puerto Rico Marine Management Incorporated (PRMMI) in Port Everglades, Florida. We'd have enough time to get the work done and use the results to show at the luncheon. It was free for PRMMI. Well worth the freebie to have the fresh field results for the upcoming luncheon.

We made a deal for special equipment made by Trelleborg and recommended by Robin Pitman. The equipment came with training and a couple of Swedes to hang around until we were comfortable with the new system. Arne Backlund and his pal Bo were assigned to Aquafacs for as long as we needed them. An instant crew! We were ready to go. Off to Port Everglades. The promised 3M polishing discs had been shipped in from 3M.

We purchased a used Class A motorhome to transport crew and equipment as needed for logistics. Darn glad we did. With our schedule, we needed to get it up and going to meet the PRMMI ship in Florida. It was already steaming on its way to Port Everglades from San Juan.

The crew dispatched from Pier One and drove from Boston to Port Everglades. We had hired another guy, Paul Mercaldi, to join the team and help with driving, logistics and diver/tender needs. Paul was ex-Navy and claimed to be UDT, trained, and well familiar with underwater activities. He was not commercially-trained but a great asset considering his experience. Off we went. I also traveled with the team.

Once in Florida, the ship arrived as scheduled. With the help of the Swedes, we were able to go to work right away and get everything we needed for the upcoming luncheon. Mirrorlike finishes and exceptional photography was obtained in Ft Lauderdale. I was the photographer and took immense pride in my photographic ability after a lifetime of interest and practice. We would be ready for the luncheon...

The Whitehall Club

Our new friend and agent Dick O'Boyle had managed to get everything set, invitations out, and created a buzz in the industry about the upcoming white tablecloth luncheon. Not only was it at the Whitehall Club, but the subject matter was of great interest Best of all, it was Aquafacs. They all wanted to see who those masked men from Boston were.

The guest list was impressive, and the RSVP was 100%. Once again, game on. Robin Pitman would fly in to attend and present; Dick O'Boyle would handle all the logistics; and Charles, Jay and I would attend for Aquafacs to be available for questions and answers. That would leave Dick O'Boyle to schmooze, collect business cards and set appointments, if he could drum up customers willing to step up. A regular Maritime PT Barnum Show, especially considering how little experience we had.

Dick O'Boyle provided the introduction and surely personally knew at least half the attendees. So, while they enjoyed their jumbo shrimp cocktails, he asked Robin Pitman to come up and explain what propeller polishing was all about and his involvement with 3M and development. We hoped this would be a sought-after service and just maybe become the norm for propeller maintenance in the industry. Robin made a great presentation, and everyone was attentive despite the finest jumbo shrimp cocktail and food sitting before them.

When he finished, he turned it back to us. Charlie was to be our first speaker. He gave a run down on where Aquafacs had come from, sure all in the crowd wanted to know, having heard rumors or attended the SNAME presentation. He went on to say how happy we were to be working with 3M and being prepared to offer fleetwide service for those interested. Seemed they were all interested.

Charlie being unable to speak much about propellers and operations turned the conversation over to me. I'm sure he was hoping I had learned enough from Ferguson Propellers to at least sound like I knew something about the subject matter. I described how we would proceed to meet their ship and complete the work while they discharged their cargo without interfering or delaying their schedule in port. I made a few witty comments that a reporter had picked up on and quoted in an article covering the highly touted social event, published by Maritime Reporter magazine. Amazing how much mileage we got from that luncheon and Dick O'Boyle's savvy understanding of the industry. True talent and a real puppet master.

The title for the article was something like 'Aquafacs offers Industry real fuel savings' and was peppered with my witty remarks. Just what was needed to make this believable and catch the attention of the casual reader. Guess that's one way to make the news. Once again, we were leading the way.

1976 GREAT RACE, Paddle Wheel Canoe Devereaux Beach, Marblehead
Author on right side of canoe

Maddie's Bar - Home of the Great Race

Author in Front of Maddie's - July 2019 State Street, Marblehead

The Landing - Marblehead waterfront

Author - 4th of July 2019 Walk back in time

Commercial Street wharf - July 1976 Harbor tour start

Brown's Island - Beach location – July 1976 BBQ location

Spirit of 76' hangs in Marblehead Town Hall

Boston Harbor Pilots vessel Pier One, E. Boston

Pier One, E. Boston - Looking north from Boston Harbor

Pier One – E Boston Waterfront

Jay Lee, Original Aquafacs Partner – Pier One Office

Charles Wilkerson - former Sub Scrub Specialist Proprietor

Author, co-founder Aquafacs - On the road, early days, Crew RV

Two Maritime Overseas Supertankers – Las Palmas – First Aquafacs Project

On Deck – Canary Islands – Author second from right

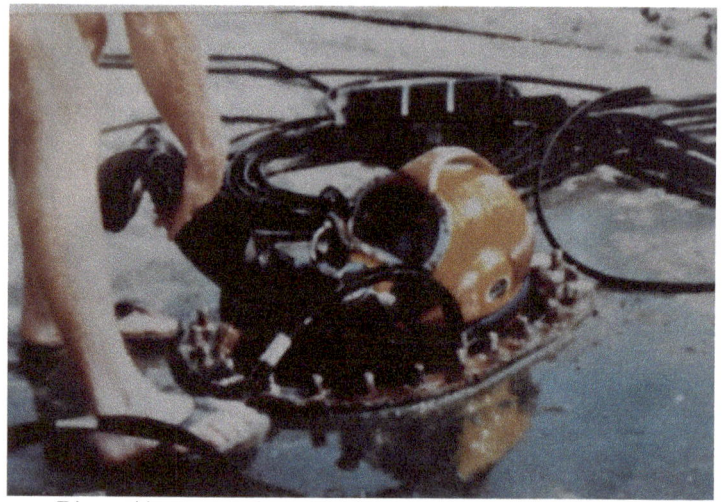
Diver exiting supertanker cargo tank in Las Palmas, Canary Islands

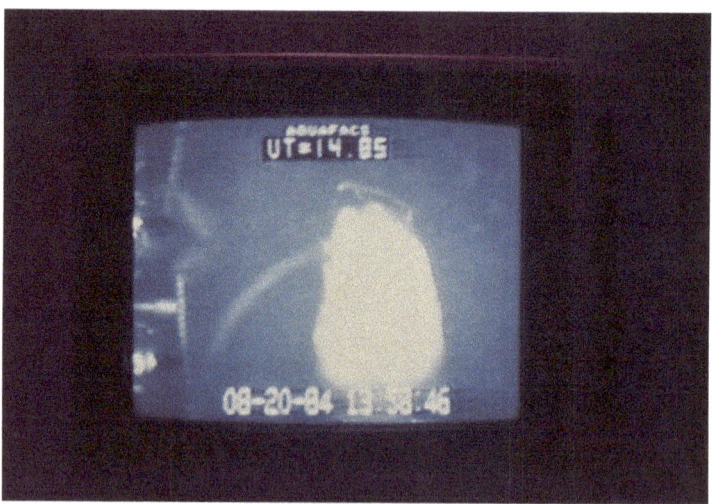
Ultrasonic gaging from inside supertanker, data in millimeters shown on monitor

Amerada Hess Supertanker - St Croix, USVI

SEAL ISLAND - Amerada Hess - St. Croix

Amerada Hess – Supertanker - MT CABRITE at anchor in LA Harbor

Author and Captain Bernie Marciniak

Arne Backlund, lead diver, dressed in for cold water project

Apex Shipping - AMERICAN HERITAGE - highly skewed propeller -900' Tanker-service location Port Arthur, Texas

Propeller Blade prior to cleaning and polishing process

Same propeller as above post cleaning and polishing – mirror finish underwater

Diver with propeller polishing tool – note reflection on blade – Photo by Author

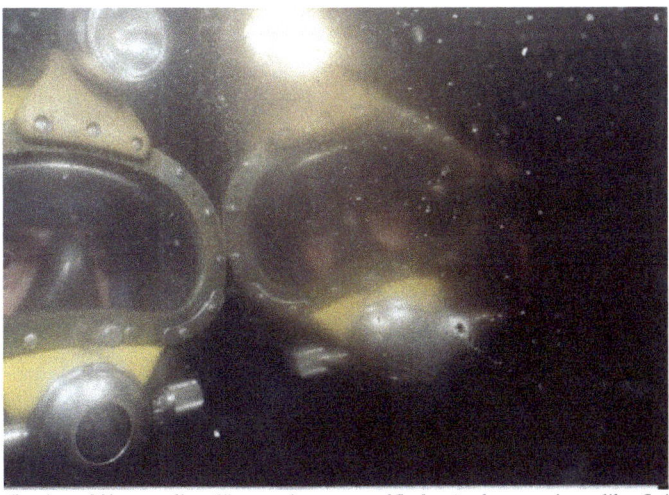

Reflection, 30' propeller, First underwater selfie by Author – mirror like finish

St. Croix - Paul Mercaldi, Author and Dennis Coleman, fishing for Wahoo

World famous beer drinking pig - Domino Club - St. Croix rain forest

Author – Favorite Caribbean work clothes – heading for the airport

My lovely wife Susan with Starfish Hat – Sandy Point – St Croix

New England Aquarium Dolphin Barge – Author with son Jonathan

Author in Long Beach attending Sea Land Ship

SEA LAND INTEGRITY - 950' Atlantic Class containership – Port Everglades

Amerada Hess Supertanker – main deck piping to manifold – St Croix

American President Lines - President Grant - Seattle

Paul Mercaldi, Lead Tender, and Author's sister Jean – NY

Captain Bernie Marciniak, Partner – Captain VLCC Massachusetts

CHAPTER ELEVEN

VLCC MASSACHUSETTS – PLUS

While Dick O'Boyle was doing follow-up in New York, we met a real Ship Captain. Turns out he was stranded in Boston. His ship, a supertanker called the VLCC MASSACHUSETTS, operated by Bay Transportation, was in lay up in South Boston after nearly being lost at sea in a winter hurricane in the North Atlantic.

Captain Bernie Marciniak, a young man for a Supertanker Captain, met one of my brother Jay's best friends after a Celtics game at one of the many bars near the old Boston Gardens. When David Keefe had heard what Bernie did and a bit of the tale of what landed him there, he called Jay and set up a meeting with Bernie at Pier One.

When we met Bernie, he said he was the youngest Supertanker Captain in the country. He went on to wow us with his tale aboard the Massachusetts as she struggled to survive a North Atlantic winter storm that finally left her broken and stranded in Boston.

Bernie sailed as Captain and left for the US aboard the Massachusetts after loading out North Sea crude oil. They headed west and ran headlong into a very unusual winter storm with hurricane winds and heavy seas.

The North Atlantic crossing was a fateful trip. Even though the ship was twelve hundred feet long, the seas, in excess of a hundred feet, rattled the ship. Fully loaded with North Sea crude and headed for a refinery in New Jersey, they were caught in the jaws of a mid-Atlantic winter hurricane. There was no way out. Captain Bernie's VLCC MASSACHUSETTS was forced to head into the seas and maintain all ahead slow until the storm passed, and the seas settled. The conditions were so severe that the Coast Guard feared they might lose the vessel. The ship was too far out at sea for a rescue, and if she broke up, the ensuing oil spill would be disastrous.

Bernie had pictures to go along with the tale. When the bow pitched forward into the oncoming hundred-foot-plus waves, it disappeared with green water flowing aft, nearly to the manifolds at mid-ship. He took a great photo. When the ship heaved and pooped to the stern, the water rose well above the second deck of the superstructure reaching one deck below the wheelhouse. He took another great photo. From the bridge wings, he could look out and see the waves that rolled by higher than where he stood with the Massachusetts parting the wave. He took the photo looking upward to the peak of the wave.

All the watertight doors were sealed, and the ultimate fear was that the vessel would break up, unable to withstand the stress from the hundred-foot seas. She'd be lost at sea in the middle of the North Atlantic. If she went down, it would be the loss of all hands and a disaster of epic proportion.

The Coast Guard maintained constant communication with Captain Marciniak, hoping to never get a May Day call. That call, if it came, would signal the end of the VLCC MASSACHUSETTS. *My God,* I thought. Trying to imagine what Bernie was thinking, looking out from the bridge and hearing the audible sounds of his giant ship cracking apart beneath him. Must have been sheer terror.

Captain Bernie told the tale of standing there alongside all of his officers on the bridge, with nothing they could do but hove to and pray. The Massachusetts would have to ride it out to survive, and that she did. She'd taken a beating like no other ship in her class, but the Massachusetts, with her the crew and cargo, finally all arrived at the refinery. Truly a miracle.

After discharging, she was moved to Boston where she sat, empty and broken in a channel in South Boston. The only way she could make her journey to temporary layup in Boston was to offload her cargo and have an escort as she made her way to be picked up by our Harbor Pilots. They were able guide her through the shallow waters of Boston Harbor to the berth in South Boston. Bay Transportation would have to leave her there until all the paperwork settled and repair (or scrap) plans were made.

Once again, Lady Luck would shine on Aquafacs. We had a new friend and permission from Captain Bernie and his company to use the broken supertanker to train divers and practice propeller polishing. This was the real deal. A thirty-foot, four bladed Ferguson propeller. Exactly what we needed! By the time we got done, it would be the most highly polished propeller in the world and maybe the finest looking propeller to ever be towed to a scrap yard.

Captain Bernie was interested in what we were doing at Aquafacs and wanted to join the enterprise. Bernie and David Keefe, Lawyer and lifelong friend of my brother Jay, were both welcomed aboard. After all, we needed people. No business can operate without a president, lawyer, accountant and ship captain. Guess you need a diver in there somewhere as well, being a diving company...

Hey, having a ship captain's view of the industry just might be the key we needed to help figure out how the shipping industry works. Landside port operations, where cargo ships offload, would be the logical place for much of our work. We had no idea how to access the ports and needed to learn the ropes. Bernie would know all that.

We were bulking up, at least at the top. Sorely short of help, especially qualified divers, tenders and general help to keep things organized out back, we continued to plow our way forward.

Bernie spent a bunch of time teaching us how the industry worked from top to bottom. There was no way we could have made it without his insight. The Maritime Industry is like no other. They all manage their ships from Port to Port with the Captains responsible for all aspects of operations and safety. Large ships sail independently once they leave port, managing everything from payroll to provisioning supplies as they went. It was a marvel and completely foreign to us. Surely the general public had no idea. The portside management was the real center of power and control from the business standpoint, but ships were completely independent once they sailed the oceans.

Most of the ship owners maintained offices in the skyscrapers of lower and mid-town Manhattan, far from the docks and ports. We now had to navigate the industry and figure out who the players were without making fools of ourselves. Bernie was able to give us insight as to how they think from the top executives in their corner offices on the upper floors in mid-town down to the Port Engineers that managed the ships when they were in port. It was invaluable assistance. Short of attending Maritime school, Bernie's knowledge was unavailable.

CHAPTER TWELVE

FLEETWIDE PROGRAM – THE PROMISE OF PROPELLER POLISHING

Dick O'Boyle called and said he'd been able to get us in for a sit down at Sea-Land Services. They were the largest container cargo shipping company in the US. With over fifty-five large and extra-large container ships, Sea-Land had routes plying the Atlantic to Europe and the long crossing of the Pacific to Asia. They also had smaller feeder ships. Twelve of those ships were 950 feet long and known as The Atlantic Class. They were the pride of the fleet and the largest capable of navigating the Panama Canal.

We were going to meet with their VP of Engineering and the Senior Port Engineer, John Katramados. O'Boyle said they were prepared to authorize propeller polishing trials and look at fuel consumption numbers. If we could prove the fuel savings to them, they could make the case to start a program. This would be an easy pitch to top management.

Our program could theoretically amount to a huge dollar savings when you spread it across the fifty-five-ship fleet. We figured the cost to them would be less than ten cents for every dollar of fuel savings. Bottom line, if they could see actual savings on their ships, we had a shot. The idea of a fleetwide propeller polishing program would offer us a sustainable workflow that could carry the business forward, our ultimate goal.

We were advised by engineers and 3M that each ship should be attended twice a year to maintain the highest level of efficiency. This was just the ticket. If we succeeded with Sea-Land, that would add up to 110 ship calls a year for propeller maintenance alone. Didn't take much of a stretch of the imagination to expect that additional work and underwater repair would likely follow. The one caveat, the trials had to deliver quantifiable fuel savings, or we were done, at least with propellers.

Sea-Land selected three ships in Port Elizabeth at their Marine Terminal across the Turnpike from Newark International Airport so they could observe. The Chief Engineer aboard each vessel would compare fuel logs from the prior trip and compare that to the next trip after we polished their propeller. Hope those numbers we were throwing around were provable. Our numbers had come directly from 3M and Robin Pitman and were likely theoretical. After all, there was no propeller polishing ongoing in the industry. I was nervous. No BS here. It had to work.

Over the next few weeks, we attended the three ships and awaited the results. Weeks later, we got a call from O'Boyle in New York. He was excited and said he just got a call from Sea-Land. We did it! They averaged better than 3.5 percent on two of the ships and logged in just short of 5 percent on the third ship. They were convinced that the data proved the value of polishing their propellers.

They asked O'Boyle to get them pricing for a fleetwide program. All fifty-five ships, done twice a year, spread out between four ports: Port Elizabeth, NJ; Port Everglades, Florida; Port of Los Angeles; and Port of Tacoma, Washington. Simple math, one hundred and ten ship calls would amount to nearly three quarters of a million dollars to start out with our first real propeller program client. This would be a revolving service that would extend long into the future if we maintained our quality service and business relationship. We were off to the races...

Fast tracking the logistics and planning to cover the four corners of the continental US to cover the Sea-Land fleet was essential. Their facilities in Tacoma, LA and Port Everglades were unfamiliar and needed to be scoped out. Fortunately, they all had Port Captains assigned that would help guide us through the security protocols and get us over the hurdles.

Time to go shopping again for more diving equipment, stills cameras for documentation, and readymade hydraulic systems. To properly tool up our crews, we'd need access to equipment at all four corners of the US. We originally planned to stage four full sets with spares to enable a crew to show up, load out, and move to wherever the ship was carrying on cargo operations within the region. With the four corners of the US covered it would give us the presence needed to expand our general services and the opportunity to expand our client base.

It was a beautiful thing considering how far we had come from our meeting with SOHIO at Pier One, to the Whitehall Club, and ultimately capturing a full fleet program with Sea-Land. Initially, the 3M propeller polishing discs were offered free to Aquafacs as incentive to drive propeller maintenance on a broad scale and help allow 3M to develop an actual product line for the commercial shipping industry. They had a hundred dollar per disc figured as a benchmark price, with two to a box. A couple hundred per box didn't seem too bad, depending on how long they would last, hopefully at least one large diameter ship propeller. We negotiated a slightly lower price than they proposed, and they were happy to oblige given the circumstances. Neither they nor we had much of anything going on with propeller polishing until the Whitehall Luncheon and our contract with Sea-Land. We had proven success and in short order. We had kicked the door down, and within a matter of months, we had moved from the Whitehall Luncheon to fifty-five ships under contract. 3M had provided dozens of free boxes of special Scotch Brite discs, as promised, and we were making it happen.

All the minor operational details had to be sorted out quickly so that our crews could settle in and take on the many ship calls. We were in the process of scheduling with the Sea-Land Marine Engineering team. The reports from the field on our performance had to be stellar.

Catholic Charity and F. Lee Baily

In the late spring of 1985, my brother Jay started the day alone in the office at Pier One. He was hammering away on the finances and accounting when I arrived. I intended to continue the planning and logistics for the expanding customer base to ensure we'd be able to cover the four corners of the US. Charlie was out of town with his family taking a little R&R.

It was bright, sunny, and nearly a summer day. For Boston, that meant north of seventy degrees and no chance of rain. There was a lot of activity out back with a couple of our guys working on equipment and the Harbor Pilots getting ready to head out and bring another ship into port. Pier One was loaded with tugboats and small commercial work boats. Seemed like they were all busy taking advantage of the fine weather.

Jay had a large mug of coffee and seemed pretty grumpy. Not surprising, trying to keep Aquafacs afloat and dealing with Charlie's financial games. Sometime around mid-morning the phone rang. It was a call from The Archdiocese of Boston. They owned a large yacht at the time and kept it at Constitution Wharf, not far from our office. It was a hundred-footer plus and quite a trophy. Not sure of their need for it, but I'm sure the Archdiocese got plenty of use. It was immaculate after all.

The Captain of the vessel needed diving services to check out the starboard rudder. The steering was hung up, and he was concerned that something was wrapped around the rudder. He had been passed along our contact info from the Harbor Pilots who suggested they call us for service.

Jay put the call on speakerphone, and after listening, we offered to run over there and check it out. Seemed like a good idea. I could drag Jay out of the office as my tender, Bit of a joke, working off a dock and on such a small vessel. But hey, it was a beautiful day on the waterfront, so off we went.

I loaded out a short umbilical, a couple of scuba tanks to feed my air manifold, and my Superlight. When we got there, everything fit neatly in a dock provided wheelbarrow. We rolled up to the stern of the Archdiocese yacht and set things up. The Captain came down to the dock to meet us and discuss the problems he was having. Seemed pretty straight forward.

I dressed in, clamped on my Superlight, and stepped off the dock into the water. The starboard side was against the dock, so I was on site a few seconds after hitting the water. The rudder did have a tangle of wire rope tightly jammed around the upper pin. It looked like half-inch cable was wedged in the small space above the rudder. We brought hand tools and a three-pounder with us for just this possibility.

It took a few minutes, but I was able to extract the cable and free the rudder. We asked the Captain to go up and spin the wheel to port and starboard a time or two, while I watched, to make sure there wasn't anything else going on with that rudder. When he turned the wheel, the rudders moved smoothly, and no visual problems were observed. We were done. Our good deed for the day. Jay didn't plan on billing for the service due to the 'special' nature of the owners. We had plenty of sins to atone for, so maybe this was an opportunity for a start.

Jay pulled my hose back onto the dock, and I climbed out. We looked at the time and decided to leave everything there while taking a lunch break at the marina restaurant. We'd pick up after lunch. The restaurant was famous for its fried fish sandwiches and was a favorite watering hole for the marina patrons.

We took our time, after all Jay would be returning to that financial mess back at Pier One. He was an avid reader and John Grisham fan. There were a few real-life lawyers he looked up to in their larger-than-life presence in the courthouse. When we returned from lunch, there was a fifty-foot Chris Craft cabin cruiser on the other side of the dock, down a way from where our equipment was stationed. The Captain of the Archdiocese vessel said a guy had just stopped by to see if we were still around. He said he wound up one of his propellers with a lobster pot line, and by the way, that boat belongs to F. Lee Bailey, who is onboard.

What are the chances? We wandered down to the boat and knocked, expecting the Captain for F. Lee Bailey's yacht to step out. The door opened, and it was Lee Bailey himself, no kidding. He and his wife were out for a spin when they ran over a lobster pot and sucked it up in one of the propellers. Lee Bailey stepped out on the dock and asked if we wanted a beer. I could see the look of amazement on Jay's face. This guy was one of his idols, an extraordinary defense attorney. Prior to Aquafacs, Jay had graduated from Suffolk Law and practiced for a time as a defense lawyer and public defender.

Jay said sure, even though he wasn't a beer drinker. I had to also say yes to the offer, following Jay's lead. Why not? This was special.

A beer turned into several as we hung out shooting the breeze with Lee Bailey. I went over and retrieved our gear, knowing after a couple of beers we might have to actually clear his propeller. But no rush...

We probably spent the better part of an hour drinking beer, listening to stories, and sharing a few. Lee Bailey said his good friend owned Carnival Cruise Lines and he could hook us up. Sounded great, but we were already hooked up every which way and thanked him. He gave Jay his number and said to call if we wanted his help.

At this point, it was show time. I popped on the Superlight and hopped in. He was really wrapped up. I asked for a good knife. Lee Bailey had a very sharp fillet knife that did the trick. He was cut free after about ten minutes of hacking away on the lobster line.

Back on the dock, there was time for one more beer before parting company. Lee Bailey's wife joined us on the dock and slipped a hundred-dollar bill in my tee shirt pocket. I tried to turn it down, but she insisted. Lee Bailey said we'd earned it, and he had a good time hanging out. Well, OK then. I kept the loot. What an afternoon.

I packed up the wheelbarrow, and off we went back to Pier One. For the rest of the afternoon, Jay went on and on, "I can't believe we were hanging out all afternoon drinking with Lee Bailey. Do you have any idea how famous that guy is?"

He continued on about F. Lee Bailey and siting the famous murder cases and mobsters he'd defended. Sure seemed to work at giving him an attitude adjustment that carried him through the rest of the afternoon.

The APL Fleet

Word got out fast. Sea-Land had announced their program in the Maritime Reporter, and the race was on. American President Lines, out of San Francisco, wasted no time calling us. They were extremely interested, having heard about Sea-Land initiating a fleetwide program, and they invited us to fly out to San Francisco to meet their team. They wanted to hear more about the propeller work we were performing for Sea-Land, looking at whether this was the way to go for them and not wanting to get left behind. Showtime once again. We'd show off data from our work and wow them with our mirror image results. I had perfected a photographic technique to capture the reflection of a diver's helmet off a finished propeller blade, creating an allusion of two divers bumping heads, a pretty impressive underwater selfie.

It was likely that American President Lines (APL) wanted to probe us for any data we had on the Sea-Land program that we had just started. By the time we would travel to San Francisco, we expected to have over a dozen completions for Sea-Land, with the crews chugging along and a great footprint for service at all four corners of the US.

APL had a slightly smaller fleet than Sea-Land, with numbers in the mid-forties at the time. Could be about another ninety ship calls if we could sign them up. Their Ports of Call for shipping and service were all West Coast: LA, the Bay area, and Seattle. Their logo is highly recognizable to this day on their shipping containers. A giant red Thunderbird painted on both sides of their containers can be seen rolling down the highways across the US.

Charlie had set up our meeting and arranged the itinerary with our travel agent. We'd fly in the day before to get settled in and prepare. We didn't know any of the APL gang, but their titles seemed right, from what we had learned. We had a VP, a Senior Marine Engineer, and two or three others we weren't sure of. The next morning we'd find out. Their office was located downtown on Market Street at that time.

We arrived at the APL office and were warmly greeted and shown to a relatively small, incredibly luxurious conference room. Walnut paneling and large photographs of APL ships, including incredibly old looking vessels, adorned the walls. The receptionist offered us coffee or water. I asked for a water knowing that I'd be doing a lot of talking once we got into it. Our meeting was scheduled for ten o'clock and not likely to roll over into lunch as we were an unknown company to APL. I'm sure they tried to look us up and didn't find much, but we were now well known in the shipping world. Everyone wanted to hear from Aquafacs.

Charlie and I had come to the meeting well dressed in standard three-piece Boston business attire, mine navy, and Charlie in black. His black suit went well with his bright red hair. Both in wing tips of course, polished and just well-worn enough. We represented stereotypical dress from Boston and New York. Not that dress was necessarily an issue, but we didn't know what to expect from APL. The industry was plenty stuffy back in NY. First impressions being critical, we dressed as we had for NY and Boston meetings. We could always slip out of a suit coat and roll up the sleeves if we had to match up with a more casual presence.

Promptly at ten, the APL group walked into the conference room, and after introductions and a short exchange of pleasantries, we were up to bat. APL started with the VP leading. He began a dialog about how APL had been following up on what they heard about 3M and the new propeller polishing potential. They were interested in all the claims of significant fuel savings.

The VP went on to give us a brief history lesson on American President Lines, incredibly going back to the California gold rush and before. They had over 150 years in the shipping business and clearly the level of pride that would come with that heritage. He went out of his way to make sure we knew who they were. I'm sure they had no idea about us other than the buzz in the industry from our escapades with Maritime Overseas and now fleetwide propeller program for Sea-Land. There was an article published in the Maritime

Reporter about Sea-Land, standard reading material in the Maritime industry. If it was the latest innovation, APL would want to get in and not miss out on the fuel savings.

We were damn glad we came well dressed. They were scrutinizing every aspect of our appearance and presentation. The VP could tell we were the real thing but would never know how lucky we were to be standing there pitching our propeller program.

We knew instinctively that this was as much an audition as an actual engineering meeting. We would have to play our part to measure up to the grand old shipping company, American President Lines, and show them the respect they deserved while still maintaining that slightly holier than thou air well known to exist in Boston.

Charlie and I projected an important level of self-confidence as our new APL VP friend went on and on with our history lesson. We were not going to return the favor with the history of Aquafacs. When we left, I'm sure he still wondered who the hell we were. For me, I knew we had done well at weathering the meeting.

The APL fleet numbered in the mid-forties. That would be roughly another ninety ship calls. We found their history and trans-Pacific routes remarkably interesting. I sensed they'd need time to consider something as large as a fleetwide propeller program. We had to let them contemplate who we were and whether we had the skills and credentials to measure up for Sea-Land. We figured it was only a matter of time, and we hoped they'd want Aquafacs to take on their fleet once they decided to move forward. We asked our Agent, O'Boyle, not to pursue anything with APL and let this deal play out.

Two weeks later, we heard back. They wanted pricing and would provide us vessels and schedules for a start-up. APL was in. We now had the number one and number two largest container lines in the US onboard. That left no doubt we were on top of the field, with over two hundred annual ship calls for propeller maintenance under contract.

CHAPTER THIRTEEN

WEST COAST IMPLEMENTATION

With American Presidents Line now on board for propeller polishing, there was no time to waste establishing a West Coast base of operations. We were about to be swamped with work from Sea Land and APL out there.

Aquafacs fleetwide propeller programs, combined with the capability to respond to our client's other needs such as surveys and repairs along the entire West Coast, was a huge challenge. Not only did we need more resources, but having crew available at a moment's notice would be critical.

Looking forward, there were a number of other companies, such as Chevron and ARCO, that were on our hot list for pursuing tanker opportunities. We had no choice other than quickly finding and hiring a West Coast Ops Manager.

My plan was to set up a primary base in LA that would cover the majority of California ports. For Southern California, we expected to cover the ports of San Diego, Los Angeles, and Long Beach. For Northern California, including the ports of San Francisco and Oakland, we'd commute from LA as the schedules developed.

We'd cover the northern reaches of the West Coast, including ports of Portland, Seattle and Tacoma, by way of a local satellite presence that reported to Boston and supported by the LA office.

The Aquafacs West Coast presence was our most immediate challenge with APL and Sea-Land. Both had ships in the propeller polishing fleet programs that were just getting underway. The ball was in my court to take this on, having spent so much time in my early construction and diving days around LA. From training at Commercial Diving Center, to offshore construction out of the greater LA area, it was comfortable ground for me. LAX and Logan were two airports I could probably navigate with my eyes closed.

Where to find help was a head scratcher. To find a pool of divers and tenders, my first thought was to start at my old school and check for resources. Who knows, there might even be someone capable of managing the Aquafacs presence, at least initially.

We could try headhunting within the industry out there, once we had things up and running. Using the locals already in the industry, would likely run the risk that they'd be spoiled by high pay and the bad habits so common in the commercial diving trade. I knew that all too well from my own experience.

Commercial Diving Center, now College of Oceaneering, was an obvious first place to start in LA. I had finished top in the class five years or so earlier and hoped there might still be friends that worked there as trainers. I called the school, asked who they had on staff, and got lucky. Tom Mix was still a teacher and trainer there. He was one of my favorites when I was going through class and really knew his business. Wonder if Tom would be interested in helping me out? He might even entertain an offer to join the madness and run Aquafacs out west.

I left a message with the school office to have Tom give me a call. Late in the day, the phone rang at Pier One. "Hello. This is Tom Mix calling from College of Oceaneering. Is Chris Lee around?" He asked.

"Hey there, Tom. This is Chris. Not sure if you remember me? I was in D-102 in '79. That's a while ago," I said.

"Sure, I do," he said, though I wasn't convinced by the tone in his voice. Probably tells that to all the fools that call years after getting out of there. I'll bet he thought I was calling for a job. "What's going on with you? How've you been?" he asked.

I started by filling him in on how I faired after getting out of there and went on to working in the offshore oilfield. Sounded like a success story until I shared the tale of having to leave California and move back to Boston due to the Reagan economy. When I described the whole Aquafacs deal and my pursuit of a west coast presence, he seemed interested.

I told him I was planning a trip to LA to check out the ports of LA and Long Beach and wanted to meet with him to continue the conversation. He agreed to meet up and said to call him when I got out there.

LAX is quite the place. The hustle and bustle are like nowhere else. Celebrities were commonly seen as they rushed in and out going who knows where, with Hollywood driving the global entertainment and music industry. When I landed, it had been a while since I was in LA, but I had no problem getting through there and off to Wilmington.

Finding Wilmington was a breeze, and my timing was surprisingly good, arriving at College of Oceaneering thirty minutes before they closed. It was a real déjà vu moment, remembering the times, the smells of diesel fuel from all the compressors running everywhere, and Al Daratany, who years earlier had set me on the path that led me back there.

I went into the school and checked in with the office. "May I help you?" asked the receptionist.

"Yes, I want to be a commercial diver," I said, keeping a straight face and making a sincere sounding request.

"Well..." she started to say, when I cut her off and laughed.

"Actually, I was a student here five years ago, and I'm looking for Tom Mix."

She smiled and said that Tom was out on the Bell Sat barge but would be in the office by five, at the end of the day.

"You mind if I wait and wander around a little?"

"Go right ahead. What did you say your name was?"

A few minutes before five, Tom showed up in the office. He had long hair and a full beard. *Must not be doing much diving*, I thought. You'd never get a face seal with that hairy face; long hair wouldn't be a problem. Could be a good sign.

"Tom Mix!" I said, reaching for a handshake.

"Hey there, Chris! How've you been? Long time no see," he said.

"Sure is. Thanks for seeing me! What ever happened to Al Daratany?" I asked.

"Not sure. One day he just disappeared."

I'll bet, I thought.

"Nice to meet somebody that made it out there. Not an easy thing to do," he said. And I agreed.

We ran up the street to Anaheim Ave to a local restaurant and bar. It was on the way home for Tom and looked like a local favorite. My kind of place. He called his old diving buddy, Willie Jones, to join us.

After a little catching up and asking how he'd been doing, I started in on my reason for being there. I avoided filling him in on the fantastical beginnings of Aquafacs and kept to the facts. We had major clients with operations up and down the west coast and needed a manager to take this on to help us with Aquafacs.

He had settled into a nice gig at College of Oceaneering and was enjoying his status as a retired former commercial diver. Seems like all retired commercial divers have endless adventure stories, and he was no different. His obsession was finding the treasure that the Japanese had dumped into a reef in the Philippines before the end of WWII, which was long since lost and overgrown by coral.

Billions in gold and treasure dumped off barges lay on the bottom, according to the rumors of the day. I told him there was reportedly plenty of Spanish treasure still bubbling off the coast of Florida and the Caribbean that captured my imagination. The Philippines had a much stronger allure for Tom. Bottom line, he was not ready for a change unless he found that opportunity in the Philippines. He declined my offer to consider the position of Aquafacs West Coast Manager.

In the meantime, Willie showed up. We ordered another round of drinks and talked about the possibility of him being available on a job-by-job basis if we got pinched off while getting established out there. I thanked him for the offer. We might need it. Aquafacs still had a long way to go to be ready for APL.

I pressed him for another possible candidate, "Any chance you guys can think of someone else who could be manager material?"

Tom said, "Hey, Willie. How about that Provost guy we hired at the College to teach underwater video and all that technical crap?"

"He's a smart ass. Thinks he's better than everybody. I wouldn't hire him," Willie said.

"Yeah, but he might just be the kind of guy that could do this. Besides, it might be a terrific way to get rid of him."

Great, I thought, *a wiseass, know-it-all to run the West Coast.* We were desperate and unprepared to cover APL or anything else out there.

It made sense to stick around to at least meet the guy. I asked Tom to broach the subject with Provost the next day and see if he was willing to talk about it while I was there in LA. He said he'd see him in the morning and try to set up a meeting.

Provost agreed. He would meet after school let out, and Tom would attend to make the introduction and sit in on the conversation. We decided to meet at the same watering hole around the corner from the school.

Tom and Chris Provost showed up just after five. After an introduction and brief exchange of pleasantries, I got down to sizing him up. He had not been in the commercial diving business long but seemed knowledgeable. His experience was more on the technical side of things, a positive. He was an expert in underwater video and photography and had a good handle on the documentation side of projects. Could be a game changer. Documentation was a weak link we'd been trying to fix, especially with the volume of work we anticipated.

That could be a big plus, as our propeller program field reports were the final product that would show off our quality of work. The other piece was, if they discovered any other condition requiring special attention, it could lead to additional work and billings. Hmm, could work, despite the less than glowing recommendation from Willie and Tom aka the 'good way to get rid of him' endorsement.

I spent a little time explaining where Aquafacs had come from, careful not to scare him off with the highly unorthodox founding. He'd find out soon enough, if he signed up. After a friendly conversation, I decided to make him an offer. Chris said it sounded like a challenge, and he was up for it. I asked him to send me a resume ASAP. I'd need that to pitch his employment internally.

The APL program was our most urgent concern. The only thing pending was scheduling the work, and Aquafacs would have to be ready. I told him I would be there for the first few APL ship calls for training purposes and to make sure they were properly resourced. He liked that idea and seemed more comfortable with taking the chance. We finished up, shook hands, and once again I was off to catch an eastbound red eye.

Traveling back to Boston would still be long, but now the wheels were turning. If I succeeded in pitching Provost, Aquafacs would have its west coast manager and would soon have a legitimate presence there.

Arriving back in Boston, I delivered the news. We had a viable candidate for the West Coast. Jay and Charlie thought he sounded right for the job and agreed we should hire him. That was just the beginning of a foot race to get equipment together and figure logistics for covering the west coast. APL would be sending out scheduling for propeller polishing any day, and we'd be there and ready.

We had a propeller polishing tool head ready to ship to LA, along with plenty of 3M discs. I worked with Chris to develop local diving gear. There is something personal about that kind of thing. So, we offered a small rental payment for the diver's equipment, if they supplied their own personal gear.

Chris would be responsible for providing qualified divers that could be trained on the job and available going forward. This would be repeat business. Every ship would be attended every six months, once we established the process.

I agreed to put together the hydraulic package with hoses, fittings and spares, and ship that to LA. Everything from Boston was put together and shipped to LA just in time. APL called and faxed us their upcoming schedule and provided the contact info for their Port Engineers.

We'd coordinate our activities with them in LA and Seattle. The first six ships coming up for APL were scheduled for LA. Perfect. That gave us training and breathing room until the rest of the scheduling was complete and more time to figure out a plan for the Pacific Northwest.

I had concerns for Portland and Seattle. We had a loosely wrapped plan that might require more of my attention. I'd have to spend more time out in Seattle to get a process established. Seattle and the Pacific Northwest are beautiful places. With APL in Seattle and Sea-Land in Tacoma, I was looking forward to finally getting out there.

We didn't have a ship count for how many to expect in the Pacific Northwest but guessed a lot less than LA. It may be a more remote control from Boston than originally expected. Wouldn't take long to find out. Things were really spinning up at Aquafacs, and the west coast was the latest addition.

CHAPTER FOURTEEN

APL LAUNCHES FLEET PROGRAM

PRESIDENT JEFFERSON was first up in LA. We would expect a few visitors from APL checking us out, so I planned to be in town a couple of days ahead to set the stage and make sure we had everything. I brought a bunch of Aquafacs tee shirts and gave them to Chris Provost for distribution as needed. I told him we expected crew and divers to wear these shirts every time they attended the APL or Sea-Land ships in LA/Long Beach.

I brought my personal Superlight helmet with me. It still looked great following our adventures to the Canary Islands and other start up efforts on the east coast. We were ready.

Provost would provide a four-man crew, all divers. This would serve as our first training session, and with any luck, it wouldn't take many to turn them loose with Provost as the lead.

The PRESIDENT JEFFERSON was docked at the APL terminal in San Pedro, not far from College of Oceaneering in Wilmington. When we cleared security and pulled up to the stern of the vessel, we parked as close to the edge of the dock as possible. The truck traffic was a steady stream as they loaded and offloaded forty-foot container boxes, and we needed to stay out of their way. It was loud on the dock with the nearly constant sound of horns and back-up warning beeps from the tractor trailers as they jockeyed for position below the overhead cranes.

The Port Engineer for APL came by to meet us. We thought there'd be more reps from APL, but that wasn't the case. Provost and I went onboard with the Port Engineer to meet the Captain and Chief Engineer. Our crew, in the meantime, were busy setting up the dive gear and machinery at the stern of the vessel.

The Captain, Chief Engineer, Port Engineer and the two of us filled the small office of the Captain, located as a second room in his personal cabin. In that small office, the Captain runs the ship. Everything from toilet paper to light bulbs must be purchased by the Captain. He manages payroll as well. The ships are often outbound to foreign ports of call, and the crew must be paid. Every ship at the time was a self-contained community. Our little pow wow today was of great interest to APL, and this being the first in the fleet program, both the Captain and Chief Engineer would be witnesses. They'd calculate any change in fuel consumption after they left port for the Far East.

We explained our process for finishing the propeller, and I brought a 3M disc with me for show and tell. The Captain and Port Engineer were skeptical; the Chief Engineer had higher hopes. It made common sense after all. Even a slight change in propeller efficiency by improving the surface of a twenty-four-foot diameter propeller to a virtual mirror finish should show up in the fuel logs, especially after a transpacific voyage.

We established an ongoing process for notifying the Chief Engineer of each ship when we showed up to polish an APL propeller. He would tag out the controls with a sign

'Divers working on propeller.' Once we finished and had our men back on deck, he would remove the sign, and the ship would be all clear to operate. To finish our process, the Crew Lead would check back in with the Captain and report our results along with any issues of concern.

While working around the stern area, we always performed a mini inspection of the rudder and checked inside the rope guard that protects the propeller shaft. Monofilament fishing line and rope was often found around the propeller shaft. The line can do severe damage to the propeller shaft seals if it gets inside the guard. It can do enough damage to cause the ship to be drydocked while seals are replaced, a huge job on a large ship. We photographed and removed any line we found wrapped around the shaft as part of our service.

This was certainly good training for Provost and not that difficult if the process was followed. We had established a simple repetitive way to work across the board that would cover all Sea-Land and APL propeller polishing.

First, would be the pre-inspection of the propeller and rudder with a set program of photos. Secondly, the propeller would be cleaned and polished to as high a finish as possible. Mirrorlike finishes were achievable and made for impressive report photos. Done right, we were taking some terrific selfies. Like a mirror, you could bump your head against the blade, hold your arm out and take a perfect reflection. It looked like two divers bumping heads.

During this trip we would also go through the pre and post photographic program as we engineered it. This was still new to us, with only a dozen or so ship calls so far for Sea-Land on the east coast. Provost had a reputation as a good photographer, so this was an opportunity for him to show off, or even show us a thing or two, if he spotted a better way to shoot these. I had an open mind.

With everything set, I dressed in and would be the first to evaluate the propeller and stern area of the PRESIDENT JEFFERSON. The Port Engineer was standing by and would be able to listen to my narrative as notes were taken topside. If there were any questions, I could speak directly to him. I stepped off the dock and jumped the eight to ten feet into the water. I asked for my camera, turned, and headed down to the propeller.

It looked good. Only a small amount of marine growth and small barnacles were evident and no damage to any of the blades. This one should finish up nicely. I took a series of photos of the pre-finishing condition and then continued over to look at the rudder.

We learned that with the size of these container ships, some nine hundred foot or better, they were prone to having cracks on their rudders. It takes so much stress that the rudder can flex and develop a crack just below the rudder pin that holds the rudder casting in place. If a ship loses a rudder a thousand miles out, there in the open Pacific, you've got real trouble.

There have been cases where ships lost the whole rudder, from the pin down, leaving no ability to navigate. What a nightmare and extreme safety concern, especially with containerships having such a high profile and danger of rollover if left without steerage, laying in the trough of the high seas of the open oceans.

Time to get to work. I had topside lower down the propeller machine and asked Provost to join me down below. I would train him up on the machine operation. The operation was easily learned, but there were some risks if run improperly along the leading edges of the propeller blades.

Once he had it down, he could train his guys and continue the process until they were proficient. Hopefully, I could rely on him for the management piece. Documentation, along with checking diligently for any rudder cracks, was critical. Making sure they cleared any rope around the propeller shaft would really play well in the follow up reports.

Provost came over to my right side to observe. I showed him the direction to move on the blade surface and then had him take the handles, turning him loose. After a momentary wowie, he gained control and had it down in a matter of minutes. Great start.

Most of the process was machine control and production. A propeller twenty-foot or better in diameter should take approximately four-and-a-half to five hours of machine time. When you add another hour or so, it was possible to be in and out well within an eight-hour day. Keyword: day.

Ships come and go and work a twenty-four-hour schedule. If it comes in at two in the morning, that's when you expect to be there. They never just sit at the dock. In a way, that added a dimension of adventure. Everything looks different at night, down below...

I came up and left Chris in the water working the machine. I had his guys dress in and take turns operating the machine, with him showing them how to operate it the same way I showed him. We were making great progress. He said it was looking really good down there, and he wanted to take the post pics. I would have him do it, but I planned to take a series myself, because I had to do the report back in Boston later.

I lowered the stills camera to take the post pics. We used a Nikonos 5 with strobe and a special lens diopter. It cost a fortune but was as good as it gets at the time, incredible clarity and focus.

He came up and said he couldn't believe how good the finish was. He took a selfie like I previously described. It was good, but I had one, too, before I left the water. It would be a bone of contention for years to come. Whose was better?

I jumped in and checked out the work. Looked great! For the first time out for APL, it was amazing. Mirror finish was achieved on the majority of the blade's surfaces. I was thrilled. Maybe we'd be able to establish a working presence faster than I had thought. Turns out we had another APL vessel, PRESIDENT GRANT, three days later. With that, I had to stay.

Chris and I went aboard to give the Captain a read on how well things went. Our report would be sent to their office and he'd get a copy somewhere along the way. Hopefully, they'd see positive results on the trans-Pacific crossing. We thanked him and wished him a safe trip...

Chris invited me to stay at his house for a couple of nights. Sounded like a terrific way to get to know him better. He was married with no children. His wife, Linda, was an RN. She said it would be fine for me to stay. I hoped to have the chance to develop a relationship and help convince them that we had something good.

We enjoyed dinner and a glass or two of wine that first evening. Chris had just purchased a new Macintosh Computer. Apple had just come out with the Mac. It revolutionized the way word processing and graphics could be combined.

It was amazing how quickly and how professional documents looked. If Provost could turn out reports using the Mac and photos from the propeller work out west, that would be great! Our clients would be impressed. It might also free me up to keep on top of things in Boston.

The PRESIDENT GRANT showed up around noon at the marine terminal in San Pedro. We were ready, and I asked Chris to take the lead from the start. I would take a back seat and be available only if he needed a little help or I sensed the need. He was a little nervous as this was job two for APL.

They did so well on the last one, and he seemed like a natural. I had to push. We had a ton of work ahead of us, and I had a sense that Boston needed me back to keep them on track.

I accompanied him to meet the Captain and Chief Engineer, like the last one, but had him take the lead. He did incredibly well, and the work moved forward. Everyone was wearing Aquafacs shirts and looked the part. I was fine laying back, and APL wouldn't notice the difference.

A little over five hours later, they completed the propeller work and inspected the rudder and rope guard. This one had some rope tangled around the propeller shaft. It made the crew look good when they cleared the line.

Chris would develop the film locally, and we would discuss the next step. He wanted to generate the reports and take that off our plate. He heard from me how crazy it was in Boston. Hard to argue.

    I was finally off to Boston. Maybe, with a little luck, we had operations under control, at least for the moment. They could handle these jobs in LA.

CHAPTER FIFTEEN

USCG BOSTON – BUSINESS DEVELOPMENT

USCG Boston, -Massachusetts

We had a great opportunity to develop the US Coast Guard as a client. There was a USCG Station with 270' Cutters across the harbor from Pier One that gave us the chance to cold call and introduce ourselves to the Coast Guard and see if they were interested in services. Aquafacs had been in existence for about a year. It turned out that the large cutters they operated nationwide were old, well-worn veterans. I believe they were hand me downs from the Navy. They were subject to annual inspections like all other US flagged vessels. Our presence across the harbor gave the ability to offer inspections at a deeply discounted rate to show the value of having us nearby.

The Coast Guard agreed to allow us to conduct an underwater survey using video and still photography to full their compliance requirement on the two cutters. Both cutters had Pot leaves and Snowflakes on the upper wheelhouse, indicating that they had a productive role in the war on drugs at the time. The ships were armed with machine guns mounted at several locations around the vessels. I believe they had robust-looking 50 caliber guns far forward on the bow, not easily outrun by drug boats.

Once we had the paperwork completed and work requests, we scheduled the inspections. It was in early summer of 1985 when our crew loaded out diving and survey equipment and made ready for a 9:00A start. Not sure whether we could do both in one day, we set the schedule for two days. Didn't want to rush anything.

On arrival, the crew went to work setting up the diving gear and video system just aft of mid-ship. Most of the things of interest were located on the stern quarter. All the engine cooling, intakes and discharges, along with the propeller and rudder, could be accessed easily for video and photography from there. With 300-foot standard lengths for air umbilicals and video cable, the entire ship could be completed without having to move.

I took the opportunity to meet with the Captain and Chief Engineer to go over our plan. There were several other coast Guard personnel in the small conference room aboard the cutter. When we discussed the scope of the inspection, they looked at each other and laughed.

"Yeah.," said the Chief Engineer, "we need to make sure all the wooden bung plugs are secure. We're concerned we have more wood than steel down there."

Another chuckle followed. I could understand the humor, but they had me concerned that maybe they weren't kidding.

It turned out that the relatively small size allowed us to tackle both ships the same day. Even with a short budget, we might actually make money on this. Everything went like clockwork, and with a four-man crew, we looked like a military drill team. When we completed the inspections, the crew rolled up all the gear while I met again with the Captain and Chief Engineer. They had actively witnessed the live video, and it turns out they weren't entirely kidding. There were a number of wooden plugs that were driven into the bottom. Jeez Louise !

Everything went so well that we were able to get a glowing recommendation from the US Coast Guard Station and found out they were letting a nationwide contract for inspection services on the Cutter fleet. We were successful, adding another important client into the mix. Scheduling would work out well as we were establishing a national footprint for our routine propeller work.

Fast forward to April 1986: Woods Hole- Buzzard Bay Light

We got a special request from Coast Guard Station Boston to support a crew that was tasked with supporting the replacement of large zinc anodes on the Buzzards Bay Light Ship. The old light ship had been replaced with an unmade fixed legged platform that being constructed out of steel required effective cathodic protection. There was a hitch, it had to be done on a Sunday. The Coast Guard requested April 27th with their support craft leaving out of Woods Hole on Cape Cod.

I took this request on and asked my tender, Paul Mercaldi, to attend. No complaint there as Sunday's pay was double time. We were concerned about the tides and timing the work effort. The scope of work required that we coordinate with a crew up on the platform while working on the bottom of Buzzards Bay. We would be required to cut the old string of anodes loose from the structure on the bottom and reattach new strings. Once they had everything secured, I would make sure we were well-attached below and that would do it.

Sounded pretty straight forward. The change of tides looked favorable in the early afternoon, so we were able to make the trip to Woods Hole Sunday morning. After we loaded out our equipment, the coast guard support vessel set out to Buzzards Bay Light. A copy of the Boston Sunday Globe was laying on table in the cabin. I picked it up, and as I checked the headlines, my eye caught a story below the fold on the right side of the front page. The headline read *Hub Man Killed in Honduras. Investigation started.*

When I was in my late teens, I had traveled to Honduras and stayed with one of my brother Jay's best friends from Marblehead, Paul Lawton. He had formed a successful business trading commodities harvested throughout the country and sent north to the US.

While there, I had an opportunity to travel out of Tegucigalpa to the southeast, well beyond the small town of Catacamas. We had reached the roads end at this point and had to acquire horses to complete the journey, a three days ride, camping in small villages along the way. Finally, we were met by several heavily armed cowboys that escorted us on to the main house of my host to be, Jose Guillen.

Jose was a great friend of Paul Lawton and a trading partner for the various offerings from the jungle. He was friendly, quick with a smile but not great with speaking English. I spent the better part of two weeks out in the jungle at Jose's plantation before catching a DC3 puddle jumper that made the trip only once a week to and from Tegucigalpa, thus the wild trip from roads end.

I continued reading the article in the Sunday Globe. The Hub Man in the article was Paul Lawton! I sat there suddenly feeling lightheaded, sickened by the news. The shock left me sick to my stomach. I read on. It was described as a brutal killing of five individuals, including Paul. Handcuffed and all badly charred from the torching of Paul's house. It had just happened earlier in the week so there were few details. I was sure Jose Guillen was one of those murdered but not identified at this point. I confirmed this later. See excerpt below from AP account found online:

American, Four Hondurans Found Bound In Tegucigalpa Fire AP NEWS

Andrew Selsky April 21, 1986

TEGUCIGALPA, Honduras (AP) _ An American coffee exporter and four Hondurans who were found dead in a house fire last weekend had their hands bound behind their backs, police said Monday.

U.S. Embassy spokesman Arthur Skop identified the dead American as Paul Lawton, about 43 years old, a native of Boston who had been living in Honduras for 20 years.

Police Lt. Maria Luisa Borjas said firefighters found the five badly charred bodies late Friday when they extinguished a blaze at Lawton's home in the suburb of El Hatillo.

She said Lawton's hands were handcuffed behind him and those of the four others were tied with electrical wire.

Ms. Borjas said a forensic examination showed that one victim, a woman whom she did not identify, had been shot in the back.

"Until autopsies are performed, we can't tell if the others were shot, because the bodies were so badly burned," she said.

However, the newspaper El Tiempo identified the dead woman as Claudia Roman, from the Bay Islands off Honduras' Caribbean coast. The newspaper quoted unidentified police sources as saying all four were shot with a .45- caliber handgun.

Ms. Borjas said another victim was identified as Rodolfo Castejon, a former manager of the Honduran Coffee Institute, which regulates the coffee export trade.

Police have no idea why the five were killed, and no suspects, Ms. Borjas said.

Everything seemed to slow as we made our way to the south to Buzzards Bay Light. It seemed to me the trip took longer than I expected, no doubt from the shock of the news.

I had to shake things off and focus. We had quite a task in front of us. My worry was whether there would be enough time during slack water with the change of tides to accomplish the task. Once the tide began to run, we'd have only minutes to wrap up and clear the zone. If not, we'd have to wait out another tidal change six hours or so later. That would make for a very long day and take us past sunset, not that it mattered with the lighting system I had. In the dark in Buzzards Bay is not a place you want to be.

We came alongside the Lightship and were happily surprised to find that the crew on the platform really had their act together. They knew we had a really short bottom time to make the jump and secure the new string of anodes. The tide was still running, so we assisted the Coast Guard with simple offloading of supplies for the platform. Even unmanned, they needed parts and supplies to be ready for any issues that might arise. The Buzzard Bay Light Ship was an important navigation aid, long before GPS was available.

Looking at my watch, I let the Coast Guard guys know we had to shift into position and make ready for the short window we'd have to make this happen. Paul had everything set up and ready. The tide was beginning to slow and when it slacked off, I'd need to make the jump and get to the bottom as soon as possible. Based on the conditions, I added another ten pounds of lead to my weight belt to help drag me to the bottom faster. Coming up, it was going to kick Paul's butt as the tide would start running and dragging my air umbilical away from the platform. He may have to ask for help from the Coast Guard guys to drag me back to boat. I made sure he was aware, and I mentioned it the Coast Guard guys as well.

Looking at the water, it was very close to showtime. It was barely moving when I had Paul throw a bunch of slack in the water. I took a running leap off the back deck of the service boat, my fins in my hands. My bet was that I'd sink like stone and my ears were clear and would have no problem adjusting. The water depth wasn't much more than fifty feet by my recollection, and the base of the structure appeared rapidly with only a small distance to tie off and get ready for the new string.

Paul would relay the comms topside as I cut free the old string. The topside crew hauled it up and tied a heavy weight to the end they had up top and lowered that back down to me. Their plan was to tie the new anode string to the weight, making it easy to garb onto. Great idea given the few minutes of bottom time before I'd get blown off the bottom.

I got my hands on the new string and rope needed to tie off to the platform. As I began to make up the rope and secure everything, I could feel the tide begin to run. I had a short line with me that I had to use to hold myself in place, wrapping it around the horizontal pipe frame where I was working. The speed picked up, and I was sure my slack was now leading away from the Light Ship and making Paul nervous.

I said, "Paul, when I get this secured I will untie my lanyard. As soon as I say so, pull up my slack as fast as you can and have the Coast Guard guys on standby. When I cut loose I'll be flying past the work boat, and it will take a lot of effort to get me back to the ladder. I have my jet fins on, but I'll need more than that to make it to the ladder."

"Ok. I have the Coast Guard guys here. Let me know to start pulling that slack as soon as you can. It already looks like its leading past the work boat!" Paul said excitedly. I knew he'd be a nervous wreck until I was standing on deck. Buzzards Bay is no joke.

Finally, I had the string secured. I felt like I was flying with my body stretched out leading away from the platform. Time to get out of here. "OK Paul. Start pulling up that slack while I untie myself. Almost ready to let go ... OK, I'm letting go! Wahoo!"

I was ripping along as Paul hauled up the slack. When I finally felt them hauling the umbilical, I could tell they were straining. I reached the surface fifty feet forward of the service boat as they hauled away and I kicked with my jet fins. Finally, I was able to grasp the ladder and handed up my jet fins before climbing out.

When I popped the Superlight, I was happy to be back on deck and done. Paul handed me a water bottle that I dumped on my head and had a drink before stripping out of my diving gear. The Coast Guard guys looked happy and thanked me for making the jump. I thanked them for helping to haul my butt back to the ladder.

The crew on the platform had their own transportation, so we rolled up and started back to Woods Hole. It would be a late night, but we should be able to make it back to Boston and home before midnight. As I settled in for the boat ride back, I couldn't help but reflect on what I read and wondered whether I should call Jay when I got back to Woods Hole or wait until morning. He may have seen it already in the Globe, so I decided to call him early Monday Morning.

CHAPTER SIXTEEN

AMERADA HESS – HOVIC MARINE TERMINAL – ST CROIX, USVI

Finally, back in Boston, with a fragile Aquafacs presence established out in LA, I needed to look at the big picture and see where to focus next on our drive to push forward. If our new California team needed support or had a problem, it could be easily covered from Boston.

We reached out to our agent, Dick O'Boyle. He had another great connection to pursue for service, Amerada Hess. Leon Hess had a small heating oil business in New Jersey way back in the day. He built that into a phenomenally successful oil company. He went on to not only build a successful oil company but continued with his love of the maritime to develop a Marine Division to operate tankers, really large tankers. And if that wasn't enough, he went into the refinery business and built what would become, reportedly, the largest refinery in the Western Hemisphere at the time on the south side of St Croix, USVI.

Leon Hess was an accomplished entrepreneur. Adding to his life as an oil man, he loved football and was to become the owner of the Jets NFL football team. If anyone wondered where the NY Jets colors came from, think Hess green and white.

When it came to his ships and his supertankers, he was quoted in *Business Week* in 1987, "The first thing I look at on a tanker is the engine room bilge. Clean bilges denote good housekeeping." Housekeeping? Wonder where he came up with that?

Not too many people have ever seen an engine room inside of a supertanker. Those ships are gargantuan, a quarter of a mile long and a football field wide. They were powered by steam driven turbines, like many of the ships out there in the maritime. They were virtually never seen by the public or ventured into coastal waters, except for Los Angeles.

There was enough water depth in LA to drop anchor and resupply food stocks and materials they needed on their long voyages to Valdez and back. Their single steam plant driven engine was equipped with a similarly gargantuan main condenser and cooled by the raw ocean water that flowed from the outer hull through what they called the scoop.

The scoop would play a major part of the upcoming story and looking at the date of the quote from Leon Hess, I have to wonder if he toured a very specific bilge, the bilge on the Hess owned VLCC SEAL ISLAND that we had worked on and saved from having to go to drydock. That would have cost Hess millions of dollars in repair and taken her out of service. That loss of use could interrupt the crude oil conveyor they'd established between Valdez, Alaska and St Croix to feed their refinery. A huge deal.

To merely find the bilge on a supertanker is a challenge, and when Leon Hess was quoted in 1987, it was during a highly active period for Aquafacs at HOVIC (Hess Oil Virgin Islands Corporation.) This included our efforts on the SEAL ISLAND, where our scope of work was the first of its kind ever performed in the Maritime world. I have no doubt he knew all about us, though we never met. We would not only learn where the bilge was, but the reader will get a good idea how far we had ventured into the unknown on the SEAL ISLAND.

Leon Hess's willingness to let Aquafacs operate on his ships was especially important to our success. I'd like to say we were wholly welcomed at HOVIC, but not so much once we came to know the terminal manager, John Fredricks. He had been instructed to support our efforts when we were in St Croix. That order had likely come from the top or close to it, perhaps from Leon Hess or maybe Captain Erik Nielsen. Nielson was a native son of St Croix and ship Captain; his family sold Leon Hess the hundreds of acres of land along the south side of the island where they built the refinery and marine terminal.

Fredricks resented us and our seemingly untouchable status as he managed HOVIC like a strongman-style dictator. Lord and Master of all HOVIC Marine. Our presence would irk Fredricks every time we showed up. We would never be his friend. He slow walked our requests for support or simply ignored us long enough to go home for the day and leave us hanging.

We did manage to forge a relationship with Captain Bull, one of Fredricks dock managers. I think he took pity on us and knew it was no accident that we were there on a regular basis. He must have had a feeling there something special going on when we were around. He could always tell by Fredricks foul mood when we were mucking around at HOVIC. Captain Bull never pried to find out what that was and did as much as possible out of the view of Fredricks to help us along.

As connected as O'Boyle was with Hess, it was also a fact that Keith Duncan, our Maritime Overseas friend from the trials in the Canaries, had a small fleet of supertankers like the ships we worked on in the Canaries chartered to Hess. They carried crude oil from Valdez to St Croix on a regular schedule and were known as the Lion Class.

The class consisted of four, four football-field-long and one football-field-wide, ships. Classic Supertankers known as the Northern Lion, Southern Lion, Eastern Lion and Western Lion were on a steady schedule for each to deliver six million barrels per voyage and had long term charter deals with Hess.

Having to sail south out of Alaska and round the horn, they had to make port in St Lucia to discharge nearly a third of their cargo into storage tanks at another facility also owned by Hess. From there, they would complete the short journey to St Croix where humongous, oceangoing Hess tugboats would meet the supertankers a couple of miles offshore and tow them through the breakwater into the port.

The water depth limitations in St Croix at the HOVIC terminal caused them the need to offload cargo in St Lucia. They had to comply with the maximum depth limitation of fifty-five feet at the dock. Once in St Croix, they would then lay alongside at Dock 1 or Dock 2 at HOVIC to complete their delivery. Both berths had piping and high-volume capability to offload the remaining four million barrels, plus or minus, directly into the refinery's storage tanks.

Maritime Overseas and Aquafacs would do continuing business on the Lions at the HOVIC terminal once we became established. The typical supertanker has a single four-bladed propeller, otherwise known as the screw, thirty feet in diameter or better. The Lion Class would add four more ships needing propeller service twice a year, another eight 'rum runs' to St Croix for work.

We built on our experience and training on the VLCC MASSACHUSETTS and the propeller polishing of the Sea-Land fleet to develop what we needed for credibility. Our Agent in NYC kept his fingers on the pulse and a low ear to the ground for any blow back if we screwed up along the way.

Aquafacs had crews working in St Croix several times a month and rotated crew assignments as a bonus to share the booty. I like to think of us as becoming Pirates of the Caribbean. Traveling to the Islands and getting paid handsomely for our services. Enjoying the islands and somehow taking a day or two longer than expected became the norm. We used it as a built-in reward for all the other not so great projects.

The first Hess supertanker propeller polishing adventure occurred while I was in LA and unable to attend. The crew lead, Arne Backlund, was instructed to fly down with the crew and see one Captain Nielsen. He would help them find their way around if needed. When they arrived at the main terminal building, a five-story office building, the receptionist sent Arne to the top floor with crew member Steve Humphries to the top floor. Erik Nielsen had the corner office. Overlooking the terminal, with excellent views of the ongoing ship traffic, Erik Nielsen was Leon Hess's #1 guy with the terminal and Supertankers.

His secretary showed Arne in and announced his presence. Nielsen sat with his back turned, looking out through the large plate glass window. He didn't speak or turn around. He was rocked back in his chair, hands clasped behind his head. After a brief but awkward silence, Arne spoke up and introduced himself. He went on to say that he was there to clean and polish the propeller of the SEAL ISLAND.

Nielsen finally spoke. "I don't see any propellers in here," he said with a gruff tone and without turning or making any other comment.

Arne wasn't sure what to do. He decided he should thank Captain Nielsen, back out of the situation and call me for direction. Arne was a little put off by the odd reception. I got ahold of him and told him to find Fredricks and just move forward to get the work done. They would do just that and did an outstanding job. Arne still tells that story to this day. It still bothers him.

As for me, I finally met Erik Nielsen when we were there working on one of the Lions. I had heard he was around at HOVIC. His normal office was in midtown Manhattan at the Hess Corporate location at the time. Usually, he was only at HOVIC if there was an incoming Hess vessel. This time, he was there for some other reason, and I was going to stop by and see if he would meet with me. He did.

He started out a little gruff, but at least he was facing in the right direction. He asked what I wanted. Being cautious to not seem like I was just another annoying vendor, I engaged him in a conversation about the new IACS rules and asked if Hess had tangled up yet with the new process.

He had heard about us and the Maritime Overseas Canary Islands trials and was interested. We had an enjoyable conversation, and I felt we made progress. Maybe this meeting broke the ice with Nielsen. Sooner or later, he'd need help down there outside the normal ho hum of day to day operations. I did ask him if he met Arne when the SEAL ISLAND was last there. He asked if that was my guy, and I told him yes. I left it at that.

"Hmm," he said, "they told me your guys did a decent job. Let him know I had been very busy that day when he showed up." *Was that an apology?* Fair enough.

I didn't do much with Captain Nielsen but knew he was always going to be around in Hess Marine world. I was told he was awfully close to Leon Hess, who always appreciated Nielsen and his family for having helped him out by agreeing to sell him all that land. He might be someone that could help me out sometime. You never know.

I would run into Nielsen from time to time, including a couple of times out at anchor in LA on the VLCC MT CABRITE. Those times, he seemed genuinely pleased to see me. Probably because their crews were all Italians and Filipinos. Italian officers and engineers and all Filipino able-bodied seamen.

Don't think he spoke either language or cared to learn. I know he probably wasn't a big fan of the food. I mentioned earlier how a similar combination worked in the Canaries. The Koreans would try and fail on cooking Italian food for that poor Captain stuck babysitting those ships. Didn't go well. Think Nielsen, native to St Croix, even worse of a match up. That's a little like kimchi meets curried goat and plantains...

I'll guarantee when Nielsen showed up on deck, he was the focus of all their attention, officers and seamen alike. Erik Nielsen was reputed to be demanding and unrelenting in his pursuit of maintaining those ships for Leon Hess. If he were to see as much as staining or corrosion on the hull or the intensely complex piping on deck and the superstructure from the seawater, it would be a bad day indeed for Captain and Crew. I was told no one was spared, especially the Italians. They hated him but loved his ships.

Those Hess Supertankers were the pride of the company. They were mighty and absolutely awesome. Leon Hess operated them like Walt Disney ran Disneyland. For that matter, all things Hess were that way, especially at HOVIC. They were terrified when they heard Leon Hess was coming to St Croix. He did so every so often and gave enough notice that Fredricks would have time to engage every worker at HOVIC to police up the refinery and marine terminal.

They made sure everything was not only spotless but rust-free and appearing to be freshly painted. They had dozens of steam cleaners and you could tell if Leon was coming, as the whole place disappeared in the fog of all those machines operating nearly twenty-four hours a day in advance of his arrival. They used to joke that they had to steam clean the entire facility, even including the landscaping and rocks that defined all the roads and pathways around the complex. And when they finished, they turned the rocks over and steam cleaned the bottoms, just in case Leon happened to pick one up. I was told that the man could make grown men's knees knock. Probably gave Fredricks ulcers. No wonder Fredricks seemed like such a foul man and hated us. Probably thought we were spying on him for Leon Hess or Captain Nielsen.

VLCC SEAL ISLAND - Sea Valve Repair - HOVIC Terminal

We got a call from the Hess Corporate office. Allan Sagretti, a senior Marine Manager and another Kings Point graduate. Finest school anywhere for getting an education in the Maritime Industry. Graduates typically moved on to the highest levels of management in the industry and made great money as well as having prestige. If you were Kings Point, no more needed to be said.

The SEAL ISLAND had developed a problem on their way back to St. Croix during their trip, after our first propeller polishing. I spoke to Allan along with Charlie Wilkerson and my brother Jay. Hess Marine had a major problem, and they reached out to see if we could do anything to help them out of a huge jam. The SEAL ISLAND was inbound to St Lucia from Valdez in a couple of weeks and then on to St Croix. They were making slow headway due to lack of cooling from the main condenser. The condenser is one of the most critical parts of an operating steam plant of any size, let alone the powerplant driving a twelve-hundred-foot-long supertanker. It acts like a radiator cooling the superheated steam and condensing it back into water. The water is then superheated again into steam, driving the turbine in a continuous cycle of water to steam power.

With six million barrels of crude oil heading for St Croix, they needed all the steam they could muster. When they loaded in Valdez and sailed south, they had no problems but somehow must have sucked up a bunch of sea life or debris through the scoop along the way. It was impeding the flow of the cooling water and clogging the condenser. It was not a total clog, but they couldn't provide enough cooling to bring enough steam online to meet anything close to normal cruising speeds.

One might wonder why they didn't have a way of keeping the condenser clean as the cooling scoop must suck things up all the time. Well, they did. What they would do as routine maintenance was close off the main sea valve from the scoop and the discharge side of the condenser to make the condenser watertight. No water in or out. There was a discharge valve on the bottom of the condenser that they would open and drain the water. An entry port had been installed on each end of the condenser that they would open and stuff a couple of skinny Filipinos in each end, and the fun would begin. It was foul duty which required men on the intake side to ream hundreds of tubes running across the length of the condenser, forcing any debris out into the other end and dropping the disgusting mess into the discharge chamber, where they would muck out the materials and dispose of the mess. I have never seen larger or longer pipe cleaners. They looked like oversized bottle brushes, nearly thirty feet in length and requiring special handling.

They must have drawn straws as to who got what end. The intake side being the only way to go. Not sure, but they must have had a way to make a fair choice. Maybe extra pay. Who knows? I wouldn't ask.

The condenser was nearly fifty-feet-long and had a diameter close to ten feet. There was a wall of tubes that needed to be reamed having almost too many tubes to count. Their system, no matter how ugly and disgusting, worked. When they finished, they would close the hatches, close the discharge valve, and reopen the sea valves. At that point, the ship could slowly make way while generating steam and bringing the boiler fully online after some period of sailing time.

The SEAL ISLAND had tried and failed. They were unable to drain the condenser. No matter what they did, the condenser remained flooded. Probably made for a couple of happy Filipinos. It would not stop draining into that elusive bilge that Leon Hess had been talking about in 1987. Made me suspicious that the SEAL ISLAND had been the bilge he was thinking of after we saved the day. Timing seems more than coincidental from his comment.

They were able to make some steam, and Allan and his team calculated that they could make way slowly and complete the journey to St Croix. If they could deliver the cargo safely, they could have plans in place to find a drydock large enough to handle the SEAL ISLAND and fix the problems, whatever they were. His call to us was a Hail Mary. If we could come up with a solution, there might be a chance to save Hess millions in drydocking and repair charges, let alone down time and interruption to that well-oiled (pun intended) crude oil conveyor they had with their vessels and the MOC Lions between St Croix and Valdez, Alaska.

We listened to the whole story and left it with Allen that we would huddle up to see if we could brainstorm anything; after all we were Aquafacs. When we hung up Jay asked, "Now what?"

"Lunch" I responded. We headed out for pizza and beer, hoping the combination would somehow magically stimulate our creative genius. Not so much. Early in the evening, I thought about their problem like a worker in a drydock. What would they do?

Absent the sea water, they would still have to get inside the piping and make their way to the butterfly valve. Once there, they would determine what caused the problem. Most likely a damaged seal. It was not common, but this was not the first steamship to encounter such a thing.

At this point, they had all gone to drydock to fix. So, what was the difference? Ah ha, the sea water. What a leap. Making a seal on the outer hull might allow them to successfully drain the condenser. It was the key, and we would figure out how to do that. Simple... well, kind of.

We called Allen the next day, and I walked him through our thought process and asked him a couple of questions about the scoop. We asked about size, location, protective grating and the piping from the hull to the condenser. How far up the pipe was the valve from the outer shell plating? What was the diameter of the pipe? We needed details. Allen responded with answers to all the questions, and it sounded better than I had thought. He had a few pictures and a drawing of the sea valve, extremely helpful.

The outer hull opening for the scoop was just short of four-feet-wide and nearly seven-feet-long. *Perfect*, I thought. A standard sheet of plywood would fit in theory. Water pressure would be an issue to overcome, and finally, a seal material that would press against the hull and provide enough of that to slow the flow and allow them to drain the condenser. We had this figured. How we would replace the seals or squeeze any one of us through those tiny ports to gain entry to the inside of the condenser were still open questions.

Allen was thrilled that we came up with something and asked us to pen a scope of work that he could run by his engineering group and then up the chain. But to whom?

Nielsen, Leon Hess? Wonder if that's where the expression 'MOP' came from, because they would surely need one when we got done, if this plan worked.

There was another guy who turned out to be Dick O'Boyle's Kings Point pal and his real connection he had kept quietly to himself, Joe Gahagan. Joe was VP of the Hess Marine Department and highest-ranking non-family member in the organization, best that we could tell. Leon Hess had great faith and confidence in Joe, and I have no doubt he'd have to run this one by the Old Man.

I tapped away on the plan. We would use a multilayered plywood panel for the patch to the outside of the hull. Plywood is considered a load bearing material and when layered six-sheets-thick, epoxied and wood screwed together, would form not only a strong enough patch but would not cause any buoyancy issues. I tracked down a special foam matting that was light weight and dense enough to cover the entire plate. It would be easy to attach with standard contact cement and could well serve as the seal.

With a ship three-hundred-feet-wide, it was another challenge just to reach the location of the scoop. Transporting and securing the cover to the scoop, located way the hell under the ship, not far from the centerline to the port side stern quarter, was helped tremendously by having the neutrally buoyant plywood. A man would be able to swim the massive cover to the install location, awkward but doable.

The plan was coming together. Allen had sent us a document and pics of what the scoop looked like in the dry. I was able to see what protection they had and how to cover the opening. I found out a troubling factor that would have to be carefully handled and planned in the operation stage. The actual seal for the butterfly valve was a one-piece item three feet or more in diameter, with the seal on the outer edge, configured to slip into a finely-machined seat inside the valve.

 Oh boy. That meant we had to open the access into the scoop from the outside and swim the new seal in with us when we started out, if a damaged seal was the issue. We would need to pass through the valve and up into what they called the water box to set the new seal there in advance.

 The plan, once we sealed off the hull and they were able to drain the condenser, was for the new seal to be waiting for us inside. We had no proof of what the problem was, but it sure seemed likely we had a damaged seal. What else could it be? We could only pray that they hadn't damaged the seat inside the valve. There would be no way to mechanically fix that.

 If it was the seal and we had the condenser drained, an Aquafacs guy could get into the water box through that small hatch at the end of the condenser in the engine room. Once inside, the diver's tender would pass a scuba tank with regulator and a mask through the hatch as a safety plan and then pass the Superlight 17 through that same hole along with tools. Mechanical and hydraulic tools would be needed to break down the valve and replace the seal. If they could do that in a drydock, there was no doubt we could accomplish the task underwater.

 The diver would have to be his own tender inside the condenser. Dress in and carefully slip into the piping that passed at a forty-five-degree angle downward twenty feet or so to where the Volkswagen-sized butterfly valve sat. If we determined it was a bad lip seal on the valve, we would have the valve closed to be able to loosen all the retaining hardware for the seal.

We had to take them loose and secure the parts. If they somehow slipped through the valve, they wouldn't be lost but would end up at the shell plating on our patch and a pain to retrieve. The plan called for removing the old seal, removing the safety taping we had added to the new seal when we transport the part before sealing the ship, and then the replacement phase would begin.

The new seal would be installed and then the retaining parts reinstalled and torqued to a specific torque value. Once completed, we would have the valve slowly closed while observing the function and seating of the new seal. If all looked good, we'd get everything out of the water box, seal the hatches, and move back outside to remove the patch. Our plan would be to keep the butterfly in the closed position while we removed the cover on the outside. We would then notify the Chief Engineer, and they would open the valve and flood the condenser. If we had done our job, they should now be able to close the valve and drain the condenser. Then, those skinny Filipinos I mentioned could get back in there and fix their real problem, reaming the cooling tubes and clearing the obstructing debris.

We sent Allen the plan and waited to hear back. We got a call the next day. Joe Gehegan was on it along with Allan and another guy, Brian Swensen, a Port Engineer we met and worked with in St. Croix. They had many questions. Fortunately, I had many answers. Ultimately, if we were willing to take the risk, they would agree to sanction the work. What other options were there? Drydock? Maybe.

Most of the risk they referred to goes to the safety protocol we put together. The scuba tank, regulator and mask were to be placed inside the condenser in case of some catastrophic failure. Worst case could call for the need to chop off our hoses and seal the hatch to the condenser to avoid uncontrollable flooding of the engine room. Sounds dramatic, but to a well-trained and experience diver, they would simply ditch the helmet and use the tank, regulator and mask to sit in there in the water box and wait for rescue. We figured no more than about ten minutes to remove the patch on the hull, and the man trapped would simply swim down through the butterfly valve and out the scoop. No big deal...right?

We could see through a small window in the hatch, so the trapped man could give us a simple thumbs up, chill out and stand by until we tapped the condenser and gave our thumbs up for the trapped man to make his way back to the outside. We felt it was a workable plan. What else could you do? We weren't going to get OSHA approval for this one. We had no doubt they would seal that hatch in a catastrophic failure, and we had every confidence in our diving team.

It was a go. We got the logistics set and would fabricate the patch in St Croix prior to the vessel's arrival. No time to waste, SEAL ISLAND was going to make it back to Dock One, and we'd be ready.

When she finally arrived in St Lucia to offload the crude oil and start lightering the ship, that was our signal to depart Boston for St Croix. We'd get our patch made and prepare anything else needed to be ready. We were standing on the dock as the tugs brought her alongside. There we were at Dock One. We would start as soon as the vessel was secured and cleared US Customs.

The agents were waiting with us for the gangway to be lowered. Brian Swensen had met the ship in St Lucia and was standing at the rail talking to somebody on the radio. He saw us and waved. He knew the plan and would do anything needed to make sure we got all the support possible, including anything we needed and full support from Fredricks. I'm sure Fredricks was thrilled.

Brian filled him in, so he knew how serious this project was and had visibility all the way to the top. He sounded surprisingly good when I spoke with him and got what we needed, responding right away to any of our requests. Even though we knew Fredricks would soon return to normal once we got out of his hair, it was good. Once again, showtime.

I personally was the lead for Aquafacs and crew and assumed responsibility for our mission. We met Brian Swensen onboard along with the Captain and Chief Engineer. They all knew what we were going to attempt and hoped for success. None of them wanted a trip to the drydock.

We toured the engine room and laid out where we would set up the dive station next to the condenser. Two of the crewmembers would begin that set up in the engine room while the rest of our team would make ready the workboat and load out the cover that would be needed early on.

When we were finally set to go, we called the Port Captain for the terminal and notified him that men were about to enter the water and begin the process. He wished us luck and requested a call when we were finished. Our first man in would swim a tagline down to the scoop and tie it off to the protective bars. We would take loose and let hang just enough bars for a diver to pass through and head up the scoop. He would then come back to our workboat, take the cover below, leave it next to the opening, and come back.

It was now my turn to dress in and take the new seal up the scoop, through the butterfly valve, now fully open. I'd then carefully inspect and photograph what I'd find. Off I went. Everything was going smoothly. I had no problem passing through the bars and up the scoop. It was a little creepy turning sideways to pass through the giant butterfly valve as I moved up the pipe at a 45-degree angle.

We had not anticipated the number of large barnacles growing inside the pipe, and I was glad to be floating along and not getting torn up. I was able to get the new seal through the valve and safely in the water box as planned. All good. Time to inspect the valve. Good news, bad news. The bad news was that the seal was in fact damaged with chunks of rubber missing, leaving no doubt that we had figured this correctly. The good news, the valve seat was not damaged. We'd lucked out. I took plenty of pics showing the damage and would provide those right away, along with a sketch of the location. It was now my time to get out of there and let the team get the patch set so that Brian Swensen could drain the condenser.

They pulled the bars back into position and loosely bolted them. The patch would cover the opening, and the bars were recessed slightly and would not be causing any interference. It was a perfect fit over the scoop which was dogged down using J bolts that hooked the flat bars above and were tightened with enough force to see the flattening of the gasket material against the hull. Done, ready to drain the condenser.

We hailed Brian Swensen and told him we were ready. He asked that the sea valve remain opened and the condenser drained. We would wait to hear how well we had done. Took a while, as there is a lot of water in that condenser. Twenty minutes or so later, Brian called back to say our patch held and the flow stopped as planned.

We shifted the diving operations to the condenser location in the engine room and could now open the hatches as we had planned. Now the hard part. Stuff someone through that small hatch and execute the repair plan.

We asked to have the butterfly valve closed. Due to the extreme visibility here and with Swensen present, there could be serious consequences should anything go wrong; I would have to be the first one stuffed through that port. I gotta say I wasn't sure I'd fit.

We got a step ladder, and I wore a lightweight wet suit and coveralls for protection from the barnacles. After climbing the ladder, I turned and went in feet first and just made it through that damn hatch. The standing area in the water box was the curved contour of the large condenser cylinder and about six feet long where you begin a wall of tubes, the source of their cooling problem.

My tender passed the hydraulic nut buster and other hand tools through the opening. They then passed the scuba tank, regulator and mask just as we planned and finally my helmet and harness with a small bail out bottle that could be handy should we have the unthinkable occur.

I clamped on my Superlight and carefully floated down the pipe dragging the nut buster with a special bit designed to remove the bolts holding the seals. We had great communications between me and the outside, so it seemed pretty routine. I went to work with my mission to break down the parts and remove the damaged seal. After that, I would carefully replace the seal and loosely replace the bolts, and that would do it for me.

    I came out and left my Superlight for the next diver that went in to tighten the seal hardware with a large torque wrench. It was critical that we met the torque specs for the valve and seal. That took a while, but we finally wrapped it up. We were complete. Now we had the valve slowly closed and watched as the seal and valve seat married up. Perfect fit, smooth closing. We did that a couple of times and made sure it was all clear, then asked for them to leave the valve closed for testing. We were done inside, for now.

    All the tools were pulled out of the condenser, and all the diving gear was rolled up and set aside, waiting for confirmation that the valve seal was holding. Thank God we didn't need that scuba gear.

    The condenser hatch was sealed and dogged down. Only a couple of things left. We went outside and removed the patch. We'd re-secure the protective bars once we heard back from Swensen. We notified Brian they were good to go to open the sea valve, flood the condenser, and test the valve. Closing and successfully draining the condenser was the proof of success. We already knew what would happen and waited the twenty or thirty minutes for Brian to cycle the process.

    Finally, he called back and said the valve was secure and the condenser drained dry. He said we did a great job and asked me to meet him in the Captains office. The last guy in untied the tag line, and we hauled the patch back to the workboat. When our guy was back on board, we hailed the Port Captain and wrapped everything up.

We had worked this in one very long shift that lasted overnight and left us exhausted with the sun up and shining around eight in the morning. No matter how big a deal, all we wanted was bed and a good night/day's sleep. I went up to meet Brian while the crew and tenders picked up all the mess and rolled up the gear.

When I got to the Captain's cabin, Swensen was all smiles. He had just called New York and said they were literally cheering over the phone at the success. The SEAL ISLAND would be back on schedule heading to Valdez after discharge and not too far behind on that crude oil conveyor with the Lions. They would be able to make up some time by increasing their cruising speed back to Alaska.

No doubt our stock was rising with Hess. A couple of days later when we were back in Boston, Joe Gehegan called personally to thank us. That was a big deal and had never been done before. No drydock for SEAL ISLAND. Unlike other projects by Aquafacs, we were asked to keep this in confidence, and that's what we did. I'm sure enough time has passed that no one cares anymore.

More on ships in St Croix

We would be in St Croix many times over the next five years or more, providing services to Maritime Overseas and Hess. In the case of Hess, we helped with a variety of ships and large oceangoing tugs.

Hess had a fleet of ships called ITBs (Integrated Tug and Barge.) They were an unusual design and had two very separate sections that when married together, looked like most other smaller tankers, except when viewed from behind. More to come on ITBs. They also had huge ocean-going tugs with inspection and certification requirements that we helped with.

The HOVIC Marine terminal afforded their supporting vessels, like Maritime Overseas, Apex Shipping and several others, the opportunity to use our services while accessing the port for loading or discharging cargo. As a refinery, there was crude oil coming in and products like gasoline and diesel heading out, mostly north to the US. It was a busy place, and we were glad to be there. More stories to come.

CHAPTER SEVENTEEN

AEGIS CRUISERS - PORTLAND, MAINE – BATH IRON WORKS (BIW)

Once again, in the mid-eighties, we found ourselves pulled into something big.

With our office being at Pier One in East Boston, we were only a short drive north to Portland, Maine. In Portland harbor at the time, there was a huge floating drydock that Bath Iron Works used to service ships. They were able to drydock and repair most any ship but were best at providing the US Navy what they needed. In this case, they might have an edge to secure the contract for detail, design and construction of the USS Arleigh Burke (DDG 51.) The 'Burke' was the first vessel of the newest AEGIS cruiser guided missile destroyers.

The drydock was probably their key for winning the bid, as they were the owner and operator and could capture the discount. That might have been what gave them the edge over a close competitor from Pascagoula, Mississippi. Great news for BIW and the thousands they employed in Maine. Turns out there was a caveat. That drydock.

When the floating drydock was manufactured, it was an amazing World War II innovation. It was designed with nine, three-hundred-foot-long ship hulls for floatation. When rafted together and secured, they could support a steel deck and wing walls that would enclose the dock and allow for speedy deployment and operation.

The ship hulls would hold generators, pumps, and all the tools and machinery to be self-sufficient in theater. It could also be stripped down to parts and towed anywhere in the world, quickly assembled, and placed in service at critical locations. Their specific mission was to be moved to the far western Pacific and repair severely damaged naval vessels battling the Japanese in the Pacific and South China Sea. Ships could be rapidly drydocked, repaired and returned to duty in record time.

Genius idea, just a little late. The new drydock had been built and towed to the far east. Shortly after arrival, the US had dropped the bombs on Japan, and the war was over. So, it had missed the war and never needed to save the naval vessels as anticipated. It was great news for America, but now what for the new drydock?

The drydock was towed away from the far east and eventually made its way to Portland, Maine and berthed just north of downtown. The new facility and company were called Portland Drydock, clever name. They were a Bath Iron Works facility on the waterfront, from where this story will begin.

While hanging around Pier One, planning and executing all the incoming work, the phone rang. It was a guy from Portland Drydock. He said they might need our help and asked if we were willing to schedule a meeting at their facility to discuss. He would not say anything more over the phone when questioned. We agreed, knowing Bath Iron Works had a special Navy relationship and might need us for any number of obscure reasons.

It was the spring of 1987, and I traveled to Portland with my brother Jay to meet a man named Hutch Hutchinson, General Manager of Portland Drydock. Clearly, Hutch was a native, based on his accent. Being from the Boston area, we know all about that, yup yup. He was a little older looking and not too far away from retirement, we'd learn.

The mess on his desk reminded me of mine, and he had a coffee cup sitting there amongst the mess. I still remember; it read something simple yet profound, considering what he did and where we came from: DON'T LET THE BASTARDS GET YOU DOWN, in bold letters. From appearance, he must have had the mug for decades.

He introduced himself and began, "Hello gentlemen, I'm Hutch Hutchinson, General Manager and chief bottle washer here at Portland Drydock."

We chuckled, especially after looking around. It seemed like he could use a chief bottle washer. He went on to tell us about some of the history of Bath Iron Works and how long he'd been there. Sounded like a lifetime and a long, colorful story.

"We were just awarded a really big contract with the Navy. It was a pitched battle to bring that to BIW. Great news for everyone around here. Just one problem, the drydock. It is so old and has never been cleaned or serviced on the nine hulls that provide the flotation."

That was the first we heard about what the thing was made of. He went on, "The Navy knows all about that and the history of our drydock. Our contract requires that we construct the vessel USS Arleigh Burke and make it immediately available on the drydock to install the electronic warfare array that was designed for the bow." ...I won't discuss any more of that as it is likely still highly classified.

He continued, "The Navy had added a caveat. The drydock must meet a minimum operational speed to flood and blow ballast and surface within an approved time limit. Portland Drydock would have to comply by cycling the dock with their folks witnessing the trial."

Ah, I knew there was a kink somewhere. I asked, "So what do you think? Have you tried to cycle?"

"Sure did," said Hutch. "Not even close to what they require. We had a local scuba diver have a look. He said the bottom was covered in a thick layer of mussels and other growth but couldn't determine how thick, as he was unable to dig deep enough to reach the hull. Somebody said they heard about you guys in Boston and said we ought to see if you'd be willing to come up here to see what we're up against. So, I called you. Thanks so much for making the trip without a lot of detail."

I looked at Jay, then back to Hutch and said, "No problem. We'll have a couple guys do a blow by and take a look. How about later in the week?"

"Great!" he said, "I'll let everyone know. Just give me a call when they're on the way."

He thanked us, and we went on our way back to Boston. The drive seemed longer going south than the drive up, and it bothered me that their scuba diver was unable to find the hull. I would have to run up there myself and drag along the 'Swede,' Arne Backlund, and a tender. I figured if we could dig through the mess and get some good pics, it might lead to something. Little did I know.

Thursday that week, we piled in and headed for Portland. I made sure our cameras were working and brought along the video just in case. We called Hutch and let him know to look for us around ten o'clock. We didn't expect it would take long to get him an answer. When we arrived, he had badges waiting, and we proceeded out to the drydock. It was an amazing sight, the size of that thing. Over a thousand feet long and three-hundred-feet wide, with tall wing walls running the length. Huh, sounds about like the length and width of those supertankers we were chasing around. One difference, there was no way they were drydocking those bad boys here.

Once we had our station set and dive ladder hung, the Swede jumped in and would determine what they were up against. I would then get in and capture the scene with still, video, or both. The tender slacked off his diving umbilical, and all we could hear was his slow breathing, typical for Arne.

The slack stopped, and he said, "It's a mess down here. It looks like a giant mussel bank with upside down Christmas trees of mussels hanging well down below the main layer."

I had a tough time conjuring up that image and just had to wait my turn to see. The Swede had located a good spot and started to dig his way to the prize, the bottom hull plating. After about fifteen minutes of listening to that breathing, I asked him how he was doing.

He said, "Fine." Wise ass Swede.

I had to ask another question, "How about, are you making any progress down there?"

He said, "Yep. Standby."

Fifteen minutes later, I asked him again, "What's up?"

"Still digging," he said.

I told the tender to get my hat hooked up. I had to see what the hell was going on. When he had my hardhat ready, I dressed in and leaped over the side to see what was going on. Cleared my ears a little as I dropped under the hull. I could see something off in the distance. The visibility wasn't great, but the cloud I saw in the distance had to be the Swede.

The closer I got, the stranger the view, and by the time I got over where he was working, all I could see was the bottom half of his fins. *You gotta be kiddin*, I thought as I started laughing.

Our tender asked what was going on. I told him everything was alright, and we'd discuss after we came up. It was only a few minutes later that the tender told me Arne had found the hull and was coming back. I told him to reel him in and lower the stills camera once he got Arne back on deck.

He lowered me the camera. No need for video. I would blow off a roll, and not having much luck with shooting pics inside where Arne had burrowed his way through the mussels, I focused on the upside-down looking Christmas trees. They would leave no doubt what we found and what Bath Iron Works was up against.

We wrapped up, and I went in to see Hutch and give him a preliminary verbal update. No need to measure the depth due to the upside-down rolling view of the mussel bank and hanging 'Christmas tree' giant hanging clusters. Clusters all right. More like cluster F's.

I sat down with Hutch and told him how much I liked his coffee cup.

"Well?" he asked.

"Well is right. Let me put it this way, after half an hour or more, the Swede found the hull through the mussels. It was taking so long that I jumped in to see what was going on. Arne was a man of few words, and it was like pulling teeth to figure out what he had. When I approached where he was digging, all I could see was half of his fins flipping around outside the hole he dug. He was completely up there somewhere inside that mussel bank. Now, when you consider when a commercial diver is dressed in and fins down, he had to be nearly seven feet tall before reaching out to excavate the mussels. So, that puts us at somewhere between eight to ten feet when you consider the upside-down rolling nature of the appearance of the mussel bank in general. That's not all, there were hanging clusters all over the place that looked like upside-down Christmas trees that extended down another six to eight feet."

Hutch just sat there staring at me.

I had to wise crack, "No wonder that scuba diver couldn't get you a good read on the condition."

That did it, he laughed out loud and asked, "You know what that means?"

Again, being a smart ass, I said, "No. What?"

He chuckled again and said, "I need you to get us pricing to clean that damn drydock. We have no time to waste."

The Navy was coming, and Hutch knew they were in big trouble. I said, "This is pretty extreme stuff, and it's gonna require some thought as to how we can do this. There are no machines that we know of that can take this on, but that won't stop us. We'll figure out something and get back to you the first of the week."

He said, "Good enough. I'll look forward to your call."

I told him again how much I liked his coffee cup. He said that if we pull this off, he'd give it to me. No such chance, and if you saw it, you'd know he'd never part with it...

On the way back to Boston, me and the Swede talked about what we were up against. He was worried. I told him that a little beer and a scratch pad would solve that. We quietly contemplated the challenge the rest of the ride.

Arne Backlund was not only a world class commercial diver but an ace welder, building ships and supertankers in Gothenburg, Sweden. Little did he know then, his skill would be the key to helping us put together a plan that might work, but we'd have to invent something, with a lot of fabricating, to do it.

High level, our plan would be to plow the mussels off those ship hulls. When I told Arne what I was thinking, he thought I already must have gotten ahold of some of that cheap red wine, famous in East Boston. I knew I was on to something.

Our Pier One location, if nothing else, had a very large warehouse environment out back that we could use to lay out and fabricate our contraption once we figured out what that was. To me, the challenges of building an upside-down mussel plow were many. You needed to consider materials for the plow; it had to be steel and simple physics, like steel sinks, so buoyancy control would be critical in the mix. We were closing in on a sled/plow design that when pressed up against the hull, could be pulled side to side across each of the ship hulls. The theory was that we'd plow off the mussel bank, and when we did, it would take with it all the upside-down Christmas trees and drop the mess to the bottom of Portland Harbor. A simple concept, keeping with the KISS principal we all know about.

We ended up with a diamond shaped plow design concept, six feet across and somewhat flattened between the pointy ends that would work as the tip of the spear for the plow that would function equally in both directions as we drug it across the bottom. We would plan on hanging a J Bar for seating purposes as this would have to be a manned sled. Bet we'd be drawing straws for that ride.

Back to that whole physics thing. How we were going to drag that across the hulls, and how we would control the sled so it could plow from one end to the other remained to be figured out. Back to the scratch pad, this time without the cheap red.

This would require serious rigging and powerful winches that could horse that sled back and forth across those hulls, cutting its way through the mussel layer. The way the dock was constructed there was approximately three feet between each hull we needed to plow. Not a lot of space but enough to leave us something to work with.

We figured we would need to fabricate float cans that were narrow enough to be placed on each side of the hull we intended to plow and had enough buoyancy to hold up the sled while we maneuvered it in place. We'd also planned to install high powered air winches, one on each side of the hull. Air was an abundant resource on the drydock, so that would be a non-issue. The steel cabling from each air winch would be threaded through a block hanging below each float can and drop down to attach to the sled.

The cable connection would be identical for each side, allowing us to then plow in both directions. Only one big piece left. Sled control. Simple, we'd have tie back lines made of heavy poly rope that floated and would also be on both sides of the hull on each end and tied directly to that end of the float can itself.

It would be controlled by a man that would be dedicated to that task and would simply let out three or four feet of slack at a time as we drug the sled back and forth with the winches. The diver/operator on the sled would have excellent control and visibility of our progress, so there was no doubt where we'd been and needed to go. Eureka! We had it figured out.

Now to let Hutch know what we were up to and refine the hen scratching that would become a thing of wonder if it worked. Of course, it would work. Hutch listened and knew that as crazy as it sounded, it just might work. He asked for us to get him numbers but not to let it slow us down. We said we would, but this was driving us into some unknown place. We'd have to reserve the right to negotiate once we got into it. He agreed, and the fuse was lit...

Now it was time for Arne's skills and my crazy design to come together. The sled was pretty simple. He went to work, and soon after, our new sled/plow was now laying on the deck at Pier One. I was scrounging around for floatation and settled on clean fifty-five-gallon steel drums. They were less than three feet in diameter and would easily fit between the ship hulls. Each barrel was capable of almost five hundred pounds of lift. Five drums sealed and tack welded together would prove to be over a ton of lift for one completed flotation can.

They would set into a steel frame with holes cut to attach the tie back lines and winches. I bought eleven cans, ten for the float cans and one for the sled as it would also need some buoyancy control. Arne went to work, and we soon had our two float cans.

We purchased the short slings, snatch blocks, and poly rope. Almost done. We had the boys out back paint the float cans with a heavy zinc-rich paint and stencil AQUAFACS in large block letters on both sides of each can in blue. They looked great. Our plan was to rent the air winches and ask Portland Drydock for air supply and hoses with Chicago fittings, quarter turn connectors for multi hose attachment. Hutch was happy to help and would have his gang hook up a manifold for easy connecting once we got going.

We guessed it might take up to two weeks if everything we designed worked. Now the problem was slotting resources and scheduling crew. I wouldn't be able to run from this one. I added Paul Mercaldi as a tender to the crew, plus a whack job I had hired that was one class ahead of me at CDC. Garret Pasterchek, I didn't trust him without close supervision. We also hired a local from Portland to assist as needed.

Arne and I would be running the sled and leading efforts on deck while one of us was below. We had built the sled for comfort with that ride along J Bar. It would be better than a ride at Universal Studios. Well, we'd find out.

The days would run something like breakfast at six, on site by seven, and man on the sled before seven-thirty. On the first four-hour ride, we would push for as much production as possible, figuring the after-lunch shift would go until we completed the hull. If we could make that happen daily, we could easily finish within the two-week proposed schedule. The extra days were added for any equipment breakdown or other unforeseen problems getting us to the fourteen-day window to complete nine hulls in our proposal.

We loaded out the large white box truck on Sunday, September 8th 1986. Monday we were on the road heading for Portland. The truck was unmarked, as the last thing we needed was advertising. We had more than a hundred thousand dollars of equipment on board for the job. Special cameras, all the diving gear and tools add up quickly.

The harbor water was cold in Portland so we would need quarter inch wet suits but not so cold as to need dry suits or hot water suits like we had to use when we were in Portland working on Desert Storm. That would be helpful and time saving, as we could use our own hot water to warm the suit and not have to worry about it until we got out.

The tenders hated us for that, because it was their job to flush and maintain all our equipment, including the over ripe suits. We needed to be fresh every morning and ready for work, after all. This was long before Febreze, not that it would ever work on those suits.

Two hours later, we pulled into Portland Drydock and up the ramp onto the shore side of the berth. We had a chase car with us and planned to leave all our gear on the dock each day and take the car to the hotel up the street at the end of each day. This seemed kind of like a real job. Home at night, normal wake up call, breakfast, not the crazy run-as-fast-as-you-can scenario with the ship routines that we were so used to. Our other crews were still out there doing their thing, and it was up to us to muckle through this one.

It took a full day to rig up for the first hull to be plowed. We needed to establish our system and test the process. We set up and chained down the winches to large bollards on each side of the hulls, outboard of the wing walls. We then carefully launched the float cans with the poly rope attached and tied them off.

A tag line was attached at the end toward the winches, and a small Styrofoam float tied on for easy retrieval. The short slings and snatch blocks were attached to the underside of each float can. We were now pre-staged. The sled would be launched in the morning, and after attaching the cabling, it would be showtime.

The winch cables would be threaded through the blocks on both sides and attached to the sled, one on each side. Then we'd find out if we had done our job calculating the push and pull of everything we screwed and welded together. On paper it was genius. Now for the real world. I had my fingers crossed, as I would be the one who had to make the final connections to the sled and guide it down the side and under the flat bottom of the hull. After all, it was mostly my design with Arne being the master of fabrication. No time for BS. This had to work.

The next morning was showtime. I dressed in and used the ladder we tied off to enter the water near the end of the hull. My tender lowered down my helmet and was hanging it just above the water for me to slip my head in and dog down the clamps on the toilet seat neck dam of the Superlight 17. That special part of the helmet was affectionately known as the 'toilet seat' due to its horseshoe shaped fiberglass piece attached to the neck dam.

The neck dam was made of eighth inch thick wet suit material that was pulled like a hood over the head. The toilet seat was attached and went around your neck from behind and below your ears. The Superlight would set into the neck dam and the toilet seat would lock it into place. Picture says a thousand words. See photos inside.

The Superlight 17 helmet's name was a misnomer. It weighed at least twenty-five pounds, but once in the water, it was perfectly neutrally buoyant and had a warm dry foam rubber inner lining inside a nylon hood. It was easily removeable, and we had extras that could be changed out, as each diver shared the Superlights.

In the winter, we'd keep the spares warmed up and ready to go. It was harsh enough already out there. Inside the Superlight were two speakers and a microphone that would provide excellent communications. Topside, the lead tender would have a belt-worn, two-way radio and headset on to maintain constant monitoring of the diver's activities and commands coming up from below.

Properly worn, the Superlight 17 was the Cadillac of head gear at the time and still is. The public has seen these many times, usually in disasters when the Navy divers are called in. Their bright yellow and distinctly shaped form leave no doubt about their presence when you see them. The bad part is that there's usually a disaster when the public will normally see them.

Time for the sled. The crew lowered it slowly into the water toward the end of the hull. We had attached one drum to the sled and added an airline to blow ballast for buoyancy control. Good thing, as it was an awkward piece of gear, and the positioning on the bottom would be like wrestling alligators on each hull. Once you got it on the flat bottom, we'd expect to ride it like 'Sea Biscuit' through all those mussels. Bringing it up was never a problem, blow the ballast and it would pop up.

The cables from both winches were easily attached as the sled floated toward the end of the hull. Paul, on the other end, had slacked off on the poly ropes so the float cans were nearby, just inside the three-foot narrows between the hulls. All rigged up, Paul would slowly pull the poly rope and drag the whole contraption as far forward along the hull toward him and tie off the lines on both sides. He would not have to do anything more until we pulled the sled under and were ready to drag the plow side to side.

With really good comms, I was able to have each winch operator take up their winch when requested, and the sled began to move. It took about five minutes to drag the sled under and into position, but all the rigging, the sled, the ballasting and entire system was working perfectly as designed. Almost too well to believe. It was working great.

When the plow bit into the mussel bank, the pointed sled cut through the stringy threads that mussels use to attach themselves. Our plow left nothing behind except those short hairs. Thick cascades of mussels peeled away, just as we figured. It was amazing, a virtual thing of beauty, and it was moving right along when they put the wood to it. I asked to stop for a minute to check the sled and rigging to make sure nothing was coming apart. Looked great, keep going. I sat on that J bar like a Sea Mussel Cowboy!

We were able to make really good time. After each pass, Paul would slack off the three feet we figured we needed, and off we went again. We figured it would take up to a hundred passes to complete each hull. That should mean we needed no more than fifty passes in a four-hour shift to meet an eight-hour day. Should be a piece of cake!

Doing the math, it would require each pass to complete in just slightly less than five minutes. That adds up to a speed of about twenty feet a minute. The sled sure felt faster than that, so it should be a pretty easy goal to meet. No need to limit the passes; the shift time would be nearly automatic at four hours each, unless something bad happened. That was just the way we typically rolled. Once you're in, you just keep going. Most people work at that pace, four hours until lunch and another four before going home. Not much difference here, just a little wetter.

With our anticipated schedule, we could finish each of the nine sections in a normal day. That would work, and our sled clipped right along and would surely beat that rate. The winch operators only had one speed, full, until they were instructed to stop and go the other way. We'd start timing a few runs to see if we could establish an average.

Incredibly, our average times showed that we could plow half the hull in way less than four hours. With a speed of closer to three minutes per pass, we should complete each hull in way less than eight hours. Great news! We could take a long lunch if we felt like it. Eight-hour days would be a piece of cake, more like a welcome relief, and easy to accomplish. We always worked much longer days when we worked on ships. Those were always non-stop until completion or the ship sailed away.

That sled was doing some serious plowing, and the hull looked a little hairy but not a mussel left in sight after each pass. We weren't there as hairdressers, so it was perfect, each pass. It did take technique. When the sled operator approached the outer edges, they had to clearly give the shout out, because if that sled went around the corner, it could and would bubble up. Worst case could be a disaster if the sled got wedged between two hulls. Neither Arne nor I would ever let that happen, although we did get close a couple of times. We had one of the locals on a winch not paying very good attention.

I would hear the story later from Paul. It became an inside joke. Paul, when on one of the winches, was listening to diver comms and would yell to the other guy nearby to stop. To halt his forward pull following a command from below, he didn't stop. Paul yelled louder to stop, and he still didn't. Finally, Paul screamed, "STOP!!!" before he finally did.

Stop, stop, stooooooop! It seemed to become a regular command, as it happened a bunch of times. We still laugh about that one. Paul not so much. He was so worried the sled would fly around the corner with me on it, and I'd be pissed. He was right, but it never actually happened... Excellent job.

We finished the first day and the first hull. Time for a good meal and back to the hotel. We heard there was a great little seafood place just outside, across the street from Portland Drydock. It was called the Drydock Tavern. That was original. Boy the word on the street was right.

We went in, and this being Portland, I asked for a bowl of lobster bisque and a tall drink. Bit of a warmup after a long day. That sled needed to travel well over a mile, as it plowed back and forth to complete one hull section, about thirty thousand square feet. The waitress came out with my lobster bisque. It was steaming and had large chunks of lobster meat literally hanging out of the bowl. The rest of the crew saw all that lobster and piped up; I want one of those! A round of Lobster Bisque it would be, and whatever else they wanted after that performance today.

A terrific start, and our progress was really encouraging. I hadn't spoken with Hutch yet as we were working until after he went home for the day. He'd have to wait for the news. The way things went on that first day of plowing with our crazy contraption, the Swede and I felt pretty good about all the time we spent out back at Pier One.

When you consider how much force had to be applied using two heavy duty air winches to drag the sled back and forth across the hull, it was absolutely amazing it wasn't torn to pieces down below. That was a real testament to the welding skills Arne brought to the table at Aquafacs. We would end up needing those skills over and over again.

Finally, we could give Hutch some great news that he could report to BIW. The motto on his coffee mug wouldn't apply today. Today he'd be able to give the 'Bastards' the news that would likely seal the deal on being ready for the Aegis Cruisers! I decided that when I saw him, my advice would be to hold off a day until we got another run at it and a little more momentum. Only time would tell how things would look and function when we completed plowing the hulls.

We arrived the next morning at Portland Drydock, and while the crew was setting up and shifting to the next hull section, I went in to see Hutch.

"How'd we do out there?" Hutch asked after a good morning greeting.

"Well?" I said watching his face wrinkle up, "We killed it! One down and eight to go!"

He broke into a huge grin that almost looked like it hurt. "Fantastic news!" he said. "Run into any problems down there?"

"No," I said. "It was a thing of beauty. That sled pissed right along. Less than four minutes a pass. We were dropping some serious piles of mussels. The guys were asking how we could capture the load and sell 'em? I told 'em forget it, we'd upset the marketplace by the sheer volume."

Hutch laughed, "Great I'll let 'em know up at BIW."

"Might want to wait a day to see if we get the next one done and build up a little steam here," I said.

"I agree. Fantastic news, none the less!" Hutch responded. "Anything you need from me?"

"Actually, there is. We need help shifting those air tuggers to the next section. They're very heavy, and that lift you used yesterday to sling 'em into place was great."

"You got it. I'll let Jeff know, and he'll get with your crew. Want a cup of coffee? Pot and cups are over there." He pointed to the far side of the office where he had just brewed a fresh pot.

"Sure," I said, knowing the crew had a bunch of work to shift over to the next location, and I was more likely to be a distraction than a helper.

That pot of coffee could put hair on your chest. No wonder he was so wrinkled up, and his coffee cup looked like a relic from the eighteen hundreds. Phew. I had to get back out there and make sure there were no issues holding us up. I could see the crane on the east wing wall right about where the second hull section was located, so I wasn't late yet.

I started walking down the drydock, and I could see the crane had started to roll on. They must be on track down there. When I got there, the crew had everything moved and were ready for Arne to start the day. He was getting dressed in and would need to swim the poly ropes back to the other end to get the tie back lines secured. No big deal. He would take both lines with him, and someone would drop down a hand line and haul up both ends.

There was enough slack that the man with the tie back lines could secure the near side, and Arne would assist making sure the other side tie back line didn't get tangled on anything. He would then follow back to the sled. Once everything checked out, he could have both tugger operators slowly slack off while two men would haul the sled with the poly rope to the starting line as close to the tie back bollards as possible.

We had rightly figured the day before; it would make sense to plow our way toward the winches. In hindsight, it was probably the only way we could do it. Arne was in and on the way. I took my place on the comms, and two of the crew walked the three hundred feet to the other side to help Arne and haul everything to that end when Arne gave the command. It took a while, only a three-hundred-foot swim for Arne, but everything in the water always took longer than you'd think. He finished with the poly lines and was checking the gear with an eye out for anything on the bottom of the hull section that could cause a problem. Having found everything clear and looking good, he gave the word to start hauling the sled to the other end. Winch operators slowly payed out the cable, and the gear was moving with Arne riding on the J Bar.

Once they confirmed that the gear was hauled as far to that end as they could go, I let Arne know it was his time to light 'em up down there.

"OK topside. Start taking up the starboard winch," Arne said. He was a man of few words. After a few minutes, he said, "All stop on the starboard winch. Give me a second to shift. OK take up the port winch."

It was all the 'Arne show' to start the second day plowing. So off we went on day two of production.

Once again, we were operating like a military drill team. It was a little monotonous after a while, but that was good. The guy riding the sled had all the fun. Seriously, it was great. What a view.

Arne volunteered to work a little longer shift, and I implied that it was so he could have all the fun! He laughed. My answer was basically thanks, but no thanks. He'd be back on deck for lunch after a four-hour ride, and then it would be my job to finish up the day after a good lunch.

When Arne came up for lunch, his tender said, "Hey, you've got mussels hanging off of you."

Looking down, he could see a whole bunch of tiny mussels had attached their threads to his wet suit. "I've been down there so long, they're now growing on me!"

We all laughed, and off to lunch we went.

The next morning, I went to see Hutch again. This time we had the goods. Two sections, two days. It had to be a safe bet to let BIW know we were on the way to getting this cleaned, and they could plan on being as good as they could be to test the drydock function. Didn't mean that old darn drydock would meet the Navy's requirement, but it would give them their best shot.

Not surprising, Hutch had the same routine going on I had witnessed yesterday. Coffee pot steaming in the corner and Hutch readying himself for the upcoming day.

"Hey there. How'd it go?" he asked.

"Hutch, I'm sorry to say we have a problem," I said, watching that brow furrow and his face wrinkle. "My crew. They are not happy about how fast this job is going. They expected overtime, extra days."

He knew I was messing with him.

"We finished early yesterday," I said. "Had to take the crew out to the Drydock tavern and buy 'em drinks until it was time for dinner."

He laughed, "Not so fast. I'm going to have to add this to our bill. Unforeseen crew expenses."

I finally told Hutch in serious fashion that my crew and I felt confident we would complete the project on schedule, maybe even a day early. But I added not to count on that. They were already bitching about no overtime...

Hutch could now inform BIW with confidence, and we'd just keep plowing along. Time to move to the third section hull and keep on plowing. Once again, the crew shifted everything with the help of the drydock crew, and once again, Arne was ready and up first. This was getting old. He never asked if I might want to start the shift. Oh well, guess I'll just have to put up with it, happily.

Day three of plowing went just like the last one. Executed flawlessly, with the topside crew getting increasingly bored. A whole new reason to complain. I had to remind them of the great food, drinks and a normal day with a comfortable bed at the end. On we went.

The next morning, Hutch told me he called BIW, and they were really pleased to hear that we were making progress, giving them high confidence that once we finished, that old drydock would go up and down like a champ. So, plowing days three, four and five were all the same. Routine, finishing one every day.

Day six would start out no different. We knocked out the plowing and finished just before five o'clock. Off we went next door to the Drydock Tavern. The crew had no desire to explore other venues. Great food, good drinks and at the hotel, Heaven on earth.

We left the restaurant and headed to the hotel, arriving back around seven o'clock. I was last reaching the adjacent rooms we were staying in. Only a couple of steps ahead, the crew was huddled around the front of one of the rooms. I walked over and asked what was going on.

Somebody said, "Check it out. We found this note on the door: *Hi boys. If you're in the mood for some company, knock on the door of room 210.*"

A lipstick kiss was at the bottom of the note. Great, even the hookers know we're here. At least we're plowing along. Oh, well.

Two or three of the crew were headed for room 210. I was looking for a shower and a good night's sleep. I'd have to hear later about this.

A few minutes later, I heard howling laughter. I went out to the hallway. The guys were laughing and pointing. Someone said, "Dude, that note was for you."

"What?" I asked.

"Just go check it out," they replied, and off they went back to their rooms.

Room 210. I knocked, and the door opened. It was Susan! She gave me a big hug and said, "You've been away so long, I figure I'd come up and visit. Only one thing, I had to bring the baby."

"The baby?"

We just had our sixth baby. A boy we named Jonathan. He was just short of four weeks old and was wrapped up in a basket, sound asleep. What a surprise, a welcome surprise. We were driving hard, and nothing mattered but plowing that drydock to completion.

A reminder that I had a family waiting and a newborn in the basket was a pause for thought. Clearly, Susan knew I needed to connect to family and the things that actually mattered most in life. Who cares about mussels and Aegis Cruisers?

Susan left the next morning, and her visit really helped center my focus and want this wrapped up so we could all go home. With that, we plowed through day seven, eight and nine. We made it, done!

It would take the next day to roll up all the gear, and I would meet with Hutch and a few other guys on how we did. We spoke about never letting that damn thing get that way again and suggested that every five years, they should do a blow by to keep it clean. It would be fast and probably could be done with standard brush machines. The cost would be way less and no big deal. I asked to be invited to the next party, whenever that was, and we'd be happy to throw a number at it. With that, we shook hands, and Hutch asked me to stay a minute.

"I have to personally thank you," he said. "You guys were awesome. Nobody had any clue how to tackle this. I'm retiring soon, but I'll make sure our file has everything they need to contact you guys the next time they want to clean this."

"Thanks," I said. "I hope I never see another mussel as long as I live. And oh, by the way, the waterline of the drydock came up nearly a foot. We did the math and figured it was close to ten thousand tons of mussels we plowed off to gain twelve inches. Think about twelve inches over a thousand feet. You could measure it yourself. The hairs from the mussels and old waterline were clearly visible."

Hutch just shook his head. They planned to test the dock in a few days and promised to call us with results. I told him I would look forward to his call, shook his hand again and said goodbye.

We'd done it. Ten thousand tons... Wow.

We packed up all the gear and checked in with our office. They were happy to hear we finished. Not surprised by the outcome, even with the contraption we had built to do this. They said to not waste any time getting back. It was getting wild back at the camp.

We left just before noon and were back at Pier One by two o'clock. I was exhausted and left the office for home. The crew would do the cleanup and collect paychecks before they left. I would hear about the workload and rest of the issues ahead of us tomorrow.

A couple of days later, Hutch called. They had tested the speed of the drydock. They had taken on ballast water and dropped to depth in fine shape, well within the limits set by the Navy. When they blew ballast and came up, there were no issues. BWI would be contract compliant. The construction of the new Aegis Cruiser Class would be formally awarded to Bath Iron Works.

CHAPTER EIGHTEEN

PORTSMOUTH / GROTON – TRAINING, NAVAL UW SUPPORT TEAM

Nuclear Submarine Propellers

Back in Boston following our Portland Drydock cleaning project, we received a call from the Navy. They asked if we'd be willing to come to Portsmouth, New Hampshire to train a small contingent of Navy and Civilian divers on how to polish submarine propellers. We were excited about hearing from the Navy and happy to help. They also asked for a second favor, to do it again for the team in Groton, Connecticut. Neither project was a paying venture but an honor to be invited. We agreed.

Aquafacs had developed an impressive track record with working on commercial ships. With our performance at Bath Iron Works, the Navy had taken notice. They were now aware of our presence and had a high-level interest in propeller polishing.

We had learned much about propeller design during our rapid development and fleet programs. The critical design and technology used for submarine propellers is highly classified and will not be described in this tale.

The Navy's number one interest in propeller polishing was for use on the nuclear submarine fleet. By polishing the propellers on the subs, it would improve their performance and even better, provide the best 'quiet' operation possible. The propeller is one of the most important components of the 'Stealth' design; it is the invisible, hole-in-the-water concept.

    Portsmouth was not far from Boston. We loaded out a small crew and headed north. I led the crew and planned to demonstrate how to use the equipment by way of hands-on training underwater. It wasn't rocket science, but it was very important to learn the technique and know what the risks wee. They were large, especially on something as critical as a submarine propeller.

    Even though we were familiar with the style of propeller used on submarines, we were asked to perform the training by using an exceptionally large support vessel as our subject for training. When we checked in, we were met by the team leader and introduced to a dozen mixed crew of civilian and Navy divers. After giving a brief verbal training, my crew screwed together our equipment and set up the dive station. We were ready to start.

    The plan was to have the Portsmouth crew divide into four, three-man teams and join me below to observe and take turns using the machine. We would use simple hand signals below as they were using SCUBA. I used our typical surface supplied system and Superlight helmet with topside communication. Having good comms, I could maintain a constant dialog so the topside Portsmouth team would hear the live time narrative from below.

    Each team member would take their turn, and after a moment of the machine squirreling around, they would master the technique. It only required a few minutes each to get a handle on the operating process. That was as far as we could go with equipment operation below. The rest had to do with propeller geometry, and although we were able to provide the education they needed, we cannot discuss the details.

After the first round of training, we decided to change out the propeller polishing discs to the finest grit and demonstrate how to super polish the blade surfaces. We figured this would be the ultimate goal for the team tasked with working on the nuke subs.

While the crew hauled the machine out and set about changing the discs, I decided to drop down the face of the seawall. There were lobsters everywhere in the cracks and crevices all the way to the bottom. Just as I reached the bottom, in my peripheral vision on the right side, it looked like the whole bottom moved. When I turned my head to look, there was nothing there.

I had to take a closer look. There was an opening at the base of the seawall that looked washed out and cave like. I laid on my side and tried to peek inside the hole. My Superlight has so much bulk that it's like wearing a basketball on your head. I couldn't get a good view, but I did see part of an enormous lobster claw. It was not possible to gage the size but was worth investigation.

I called the gang topside and said, "Hello topside. Don't know if you Navy guys like lobsters but there's a huge lobster down here at the base of the seawall. If I didn't have this damn hardhat on, I'd go in after it. I'll leave a marker pointing at the location in case any of you dare to go after it."

Then, I asked my tender to take up my slack. I decided to clear the area if there was about to be a dozen Navy divers swirling around down here after the challenge. When I reached the deck and unclamped my Superlight, there were no Navy divers on deck.

My tender was laughing. He said, "As soon as you told them about that lobster, they all razzed each other and jumped in to see who would get it first!"

Guess we'd find out. I asked for a bottle of water and waited to see what came up. After five minutes or so, the Navy guys started to surface and climb out. They were all hooting and laughing.

One of them said, "Goddamn, that was the biggest son of a bitch lobster I've ever seen! I bet that thing weighs 50 pounds!"

"Well, where is it?" I asked

Another Navy guy said, "No way. That thing could bite your hand off if it got ahold of you!"

"And you call yourself Navy Divers?" I said. "If I didn't have this damn hardhat on, I'd climb right inside that hole and yank that son of a bitch out of there!"

They howled laughing while asking if I wanted to borrow their scuba gear.

"No can do. Company policy wouldn't allow it, but if I could, that lobster would be right here on deck!"

That brought another round of laughing and razzing from the Navy guys...

Back to business. We went another round below with the fine abrasives, and each guy was once again shown the method and control needed to achieve a super polish finish, mirrorlike. They did an excellent job, and we were done for the day.

We spent about four hours with the team before rolling up and heading back to Boston. They were happy with the session at Portsmouth, and we were looking forward to the upcoming schedule for Groton.

Groton

Two weeks following our Portsmouth trip, we were on our way to Groton, Connecticut. Besides a much longer ride, we followed the same plan as we had in Portsmouth. We were met by the team, and it was an instant replay. Once again, they provided a large support vessel, and it was showtime.

We were able to roll up and make it back on the same day to Boston. The Navy had what it needed. They would move forward from there, acquiring the machinery and abrasives from 3M to set up their teams. I would bet that every submarine and large Naval ship has an ongoing program for propeller polishing to this day.

CHAPTER NINETEEN

NEW ENGLAND AQUARIUM – DOLPHIN HABITAT RESTORATION

While we were up in Portland, wrapping up the Bath Iron Works and Portland Drydock project, our office got a call from the New England Aquarium. It was right across the harbor from us at Pier One. They had a problem.

The Aquarium owned and operated a floating dolphin habitat. The habitat not only served for where the dolphins lived but contained a show tank auditorium. The dolphins had a schedule to come out every day, meet the crowds, and perform to the cheers of the patrons. They were incredibly popular and a huge draw for the Aquarium.

The barge that housed the dolphins was named DISCOVERY. It was a large, multi-story venue with an observation deck on top for people to take in views and the salty air on the Boston waterfront. The sun shines to some degree just over fifty percent of the time. The rest, that famous slate gray cloud layer, that if you didn't know the sky was blue, you'd think it was gray due to a total lack of any discernable form. Clouds are supposed to have form, come and go, but not so in Boston. The gray layer blots out the sun for days at a time. At least the observation deck of the barge provided visitors an unobstructed view of the harbor, and gray sky or not, it was an excellent place to enjoy the waterfront experience.

The barge was painted gray and the upper structure white with large dark blue medallions and three leaping dolphins on each side. It was truly a great looking addition to the already highly acclaimed New England Aquarium.

We had previously worked at the Aquarium repairing the mooring dolphins, two structures that held the barge in place. There were problems with the hardware below the waterline, and it required high pressure water blasting underwater to clear off the marine growth to make the repairs and replace the hardware. The work had gone flawlessly, and we made a friend in their Chief Engineer Jimmy. He knew we had experience, and he was confident we could be trusted. This was an extremely sensitive issue and had to be addressed right away.

Personally, I loved the Aquarium. As a kid, I used to go there along with the Museum of Science down on the Charles River. Everyone came to see the dolphins. Their trainers and caretakers were dedicated and did double duty. They had a highly active animal rescue and marine mammal rehab center around the backside of the main building. If pilot whales beached on the south side of Cape Cod somewhere, it would be this gang that would lead the charge to rescue the animals and bring them back to Boston for treatment.

What brought us back was a problem below deck out of the view of the public. They were in danger of losing their operating permit for the dolphin shows. Recently, they had failed their periodic inspection of the barge due to the condition of the dolphin habitat. The habitat was located behind and under the auditorium and was visibly showing rust and peeling coatings. The argument was that the dolphins could be at risk of injury or worse if they scuffed against the bad spots or happened to ingest pieces of the epoxy paint that was flaking off in good sized patches, even though it was rated non-toxic.

    They were given a short amount of time to come up with an action plan and remediation. Without that, they would be required to shut down the dolphin shows. That was not only their prime attraction but drove the crowds and revenue stream, much of that was used for research and rescues. That would be unimaginable and totally unacceptable. We had to help them if we could. I guess we were now in the underwater painting business.

    New England Aquarium was not the only aquarium with a dolphin habitat, albeit the unique floating habitat and design. Jimmy asked us if we were willing to meet him and his Director to help brainstorm how to tackle this. We agreed, and Charlie and I went over there the next day. We were in for an earful.

    Jimmy gave us the rundown while the Director listened. This was clearly out of the Directors area of expertise, other than to support Jimmy in any way possible. When you're talking about NE Aquarium Dolphins, there was a possibility of this becoming a political football if it became a public issue. They needed to quickly and quietly resolve the problem.

    Boston was good for political footballs. Think Big Dig, third harbor tunnel project, and other special projects seemingly managed by Italian and Irish owned construction companies. We'll leave it at that. I have a terrific side story for another time about the engineering and lead up to the tunnel...

Back to the dolphins. Jimmy had already done a bunch of leg work on remedial coatings for dolphin habitats. This project was unique due to the barge and more of a wet work environment than any other. He found a new product called Aquatapoxy, a two-part epoxy coating that was certified non-toxic. Perfect for dolphins and marine mammal habitats. Their unique sales pitch included the ability of painting the material underwater. It had been used successfully to repair similar issues to the New England Aquarium with a couple of exceptions. The work was done in the dry, with plenty of time to prep and complete the repairs and enough drying time before the dolphins would move back in. We would not have the luxury of time here, but what was that painting underwater thing?

The dolphins could be moved to the auditorium tank, allowing us to drain and access the areas that needed the fix, but they were limited in the amount of time they could stay there. Could be a big problem. The other issue was whether we could schedule the repair, with multiple visits, as in two or three consecutive night shifts. Any of the work would have to be done after hours due to public access during the day. Huh, another night job. We were getting good at those.

We finished up the meeting and left with an action item to get back with Jimmy after digging a little deeper into Aquatapoxy. He gave us contact information and a general office phone number. We told him we'd make a call to see whether their product could actually be painted underwater. I love a challenge, and lives were at stake here, dolphin lives.

I called Aquatapoxy and they hooked me up with their rep for the Boston area. Their rep was way more than a sales guy and had been intimately involved with other dolphin habitat projects around the country. He viewed his job as a mission more than a sales job. In this case, we needed that kind of a guy to help pull us through the project. His name was Steve, not sure if I ever knew his last name, but he was an Aquatapoxy expert. Thanks to him, we were also going to become experts!

When I described what we were up against, he scheduled to make the trip to Boston within a day of my call and wanted to get right in to see how bad things were. I had a bunch of questions for Steve but decided to wait until he came to town so both Jimmy and I could hear what he had to say.

When Jimmy heard we were on the way in a couple of days to assess the condition, he said he'd arrange to have the dolphins moved to the main show tank. If they were out of the habitat area, the water clarity would be excellent and not stirred up by the dolphins flipping around while we checked out the condition. The damage should be easy to see. Sounded like a plan.

Steve faxed over information and spec sheets for Aquatapoxy. It helpfully touched on pre-work prep and recommended application for the material. I had a couple of questions, and if we got the right answers, this just might work. Most importantly was drying time, and in our case, it may come down to something called skin factor, the point where the material is dry to the touch and will not transfer if bumped against while not being completely cured. They did say it could be applied underwater, so it must cure in the wet. The second was how fast the material would skin over and could that be accelerated somehow.

My hope was that with limited out of tank time for the dolphins, that would allow us enough time to drain the habitat, prep, and recoat the damaged areas. The new coating would have to be skinned over before the dolphins could be returned to the habitat tank.

We arranged to meet Steve at the Aquarium around ten in the morning and let Jimmy know to have the trainers move the dolphins. We'd meet in the Aquarium lobby, see Jimmy and his Director to discuss Aquatapoxy, and outline our high-level plan to prep and recoat the bad spots.

Steve showed up, and Charlie and I spent a couple of minutes with him before heading up to the Directors office, discussing what kind of a plan we had in mind. We needed him onboard or to let us know if we were out of line before we stepped in it. Our plan was to look at this as a two-night event.

The first night, we'd drain the tank and prep everything in the habitat tank. We'd clean up our mess and reflood the habitat. The dolphins could return and though they might be curious at the changes in the tank there was no real risk of injury and may even be safer than before the prep. The second night, we'd drain the tank again, use high velocity fans to blow dry the tank area for an hour or so, and then mix and apply the material using fat knap rollers and large paint brushes. Steve said he thought that could work.

Before we headed up, I had one more important question. Skin time and risk of transfer of material potential should the dolphin bump into newly coated patches in the habitat tank was a huge concern. He said the safest way to accelerate the skin time would be the high velocity fans. There was still a question as to whether the dolphins would rub against the material and cause a transfer. I could see it now, painted dolphins, the new show...

Up we went to see Jimmy and the Director. I wouldn't mention transfer potential unless asked directly and hope my answer was right. The material was non-toxic after all. I was afraid to ask Steve how long it might take for Aquatapoxy to wear off a dolphin. Look at the bright side, maybe they'd be easier to ID with a paint swath. I'd keep that one to myself.

Jimmy and the Director greeted us at the door to a small conference room upstairs at the Aquarium. I filled them in on my conversation with Steve and asked that Steve speak up about Aquatapoxy, including where they had used it for dolphin habitats and other coatings where non-toxic coatings were required, such as inside public works water towers. He spent nearly twenty minutes speaking about the merits of his product and the ease of use.

Actual projects and results were brought up and evoked spontaneous question and answer sessions along the way. I quizzed him on the underwater application they had claimed and brought up the skin time issue we discussed. He confirmed that Aquatapoxy could be painted underwater, but it required a special technique, not sure what that meant. We were planning for all of the repair work and painting in the dry, but the habitat would be filled with water before it was cured.

Steve finished up and turned it back to us. Charlie and I had kicked our plan around and felt pretty good about it. He fancied himself a bit of a marine biologist and wanted to be more involved than usual with the project. OK by me, if he didn't get too much in the way. This one was going to get messy. We left it that Steve was going to get us the answers on skin time and the acceleration of the drying time process.

We likely needed both to work due to our extreme time constraints. The trainers for the dolphins felt we risked the animals' health if we confined them in the show tank too long at a stretch; they were looking at seven to eight hours max. It they were too stressed, they would have to postpone the shows until we finished. We figured there was a high possibility that they may not perform while we rattled our way through this. We would recommend that the aquarium simply postpone their shows for a couple of days while we completed the work. It may take a day or two to get them back performing again. The public could still have access to the observation deck on the barge. What other choices did they have?

At the beginning of the following week, we heard back from Steve and got the answers we needed to proceed. The skin time was not much more than an hour, and if we had good air circulation, he felt we could get by without using an accelerator. Great news. If we went with the two-night plan we had discussed with Jimmy and the Director, we had a good shot. We set up a conference call with the Aquarium to discuss.

Jimmy set up the call for us, and when we all joined, I asked Steve to fill everyone in on his finding. Then, we would discuss the way forward. When they heard the skin-time was around an hour without accelerators, Jimmy knew we could make this work.

My turn. Charlie was in the office but knew I would have to lead the call for Aquafacs. I told the group we were a go to work with the Aquarium, if they agreed. Steve chimed in and said he planned to attend in case we needed any 'technical' assistance. We were happy to hear that; I'll bet he wanted to be there to pitch in and add it to his resume. It wouldn't hurt his Aquatapoxy sales either. I said it sounded like a great idea and thanked him. We'd be happy to have him there for his expertise.

Jimmy said he and the Director would have to run it past the Board but were confident we had a workable solution. The board met once a month. The next meeting was in a week or so. There was at least one thing working in our favor, the weather.

It was late spring in Boston. The temperatures were rising, and the rains had settled down as summer approached. Mid-June was a special time, public schools had just wrapped up for the year and families were planning for summer vacations. The Aquarium provided a special, local place for kids and families to visit, and the dolphins were the stars of the show.

With the weather improving, common sense would dictate that our skin time for Aquatapoxy would be approaching its shortest time. Really good news. I hated the idea of painted dolphins. We needed to get our work done as soon as possible, if they approved.

The board of New England Aquarium met and had a consensus. They agreed with Jimmy, trusted him to manage things on their behalf, and gave their approval to proceed as we planned. All the scheduling and fine tuning would be done together with Jimmy, Aquafacs, and support from Aquatapoxy. Their product was key. It had to work as promised. We were going to take Steve up on his offer to attend. We were not paint experts by any stretch of the imagination.

Jimmy checked in with his dolphin trainers and the business side of the house to pick the best two-day window during the week to plan the project. They would postpone the dolphin shows for the two days to manage their stress. The trainers were concerned but told Jimmy they could get the dolphins to settle down and get back to what they did best, perform for their friends that came every day to see them and cheer them on. It would be a Tuesday and Wednesday night window. Our crew would pre-stage materials, tools and all things needed to get the job done at Pier One ahead of the roll out, giving us breathing room to inventory everything. No Home Depot runs in the middle of the night.

So Aquafacs had now become a painting company. There was no diving involved with this one. Despite that, we had no lack of enthusiasm from our crew. They were pumped up; saving the dolphins gave them a special sense of purpose. We all felt that. Time to get on the coveralls.

The Fourth of July was a Monday in 1988. So, the two nights following directly on the heels of the holiday made a lot a sense. Visitor numbers would be down some, and for those that did show up, the Aquarium clearly had posted the notice with good spin. They were renovating the dolphin's home and readying for a great summer show.

The Fourth came, and the temperature, true to Boston, had dropped off dramatically. Somehow a cold front showed up to put a chill on the holiday. You needed a jacket and a blanket to catch the world-famous fireworks and Boston Pops display on the Charles River. That certainly wouldn't help our drying time to get the coating skin set. We'd just have to hope things warmed up a bit on Tuesday.

The schedule might have to be moved forward a couple of hours to drain the habitat earlier before the evening chill set in. Tuesday night was all prep, so we looked to Wednesday night's forecast for the real showtime. Weather forecasts called for things to warm up Wednesday to typical temperatures for early July, highs in the seventies to low eighties. We hoped they were right.

Tuesday afternoon, we moved all our gear to the dolphin barge. We had a six-man crew and plenty of tools and supplies to tackle the prep work. We would start draining the tank at six p.m. and start the high velocity fans right away. Our tools would work if the areas were still damp, but the dryer the better to speed up the process.

The patches ranged from a square foot to more than a square yard (nine square feet,) and there were a bunch of them throughout. We had a few complaints from crew members about the smell in the habitat area. There was definitely a funky smell, like a musty and fishy kind of thing. It was obnoxious for sure, if you thought about it, but we didn't have time to think, let alone be concerned if it was a little fishy in there.

The pumps for draining the tanks were high capacity. They never knew if there would be a critical need, but with the Aquariums rescue program, they figured it was a sound investment to have them at the ready. The faster the better. They claimed they could drain the tank in about twenty minutes. Filling only took slightly longer due to filtering. Both played into our schedule to minimize the out-of-habitat time for the dolphins.

The trainers moved the dolphins into the auditorium show tank, and we started the pumps. You could see the water level drop from minute to minute as the pumps whirred. They pumped out the last of it in just under twenty minutes as predicted.

We set up the fans and started laying everything out as the fans blew in all directions inside the tank. They were set strategically on the bottom of the tank and blowing everything back toward the main drain. Thirty minutes later, we were hard at it. The crew had a combination of grinders and needle guns to clean up pitted or more corroded spots. We had a spotter, me, with a marker to ID the roughest spots and help direct the best use of our tools and crew. A regular ballet of steel preparation.

Jimmy checked with the trainers on how the dolphins were handling the noise. All that rattling and grinding would resonate in the water and we worried it could set them off and create panic. Fortunately, they were able to keep them calm enough. Maybe they bribed them with fish treats if they got overly riled.

By two a.m. on Wednesday morning, we had finished the prep work and gotten to the cleanup. We had large shop vacs and brooms. After we got off as much as possible, we set up a fire hose and sprayed off any remaining small bits. They'd be washed down to the area of the main drain and were discharged by intermittent on and off cycling on the pump. After all, everything we removed was non-toxic or fine particles of scale and rust that we didn't consider polluting anything in Boston Harbor.

By around four a.m., we were finished and packing up the prep tools. We'd leave them rolled up in the corner and get going. Rest would be essential for later that same evening. The tank looked terrible with all the bare patches and blotches. Oh well, it would be a different story by this time the next day...

They turned the fill pumps back on and the tank was beginning to fill as we left. The dolphins would be returned to the habitat within an hour or so of our departure. Day one was completed as planned. A relief for sure.

Wednesday afternoon, we regrouped and got ready for a long night of mixing epoxy paint and getting all the areas we prepped up well-coated. The sooner we started applying the Aquatapoxy, the sooner the material would set up. Steve recommended we have twenty gallons on hand and agreed to take back any of the unused material. At over a hundred bucks a gallon, it added up fast.

The product was supplied in gallon cans, making it easy to handle. Being a two-part mix, we had to be speedy with getting each gallon well mixed while being careful not to get too far ahead and risk exceeding the pot life. The epoxy paint could start setting up and wreck the gallon batch. Probably why Steve suggested we have twenty gallons just in case, figuring we'd wreck a gallon or two along the way.

We brought enough fat knap rollers and heavy duty four-inch brushes to maximize coverage and minimize time per gallon when we started. There was no way to use a spray gun due to how thick the material was and its inability to thin it out.

First things first. Time to move the dolphins to the auditorium show tank and start draining the habitat. For tonight's painting party, we'd have to hose down the tank with fresh water to make sure we removed as much salt as possible before applying the epoxy paint.

Once the tank was drained, we used four large diameter garden hoses with high volume spray nozzles for the wash down and did the intermittent drain thing again to flush the fresh water. When we finished, the fans were reset like the night before and the drying began.

Steve said the longer we could wait, the better. Even though Aquatapoxy can be applied to a wet surface, it didn't adhere as well and took longer to apply, a fact we would come to find out on our next adventure at the Aquarium. We gave it an hour head start with the fan, and after we determined the vertical sides were dry enough to the touch, started mixing the Aquatapoxy. We had a nine by twelve canvas tarp where all the paint cans and mixing tools were set. This was going to be messy, and the tarp would hopefully contain any spillage.

We assigned four of the crew as painters, two with brushes and two with rollers. The other two of us would mix material and help the teams stay supplied with paint and fresh rollers or brushes if they needed them. The teams would start from opposite sides and work back toward the middle. There was enough room to move around the patches on the bottom if you were careful not to step in fresh epoxy paint. The bottom would be last. We'd paint our way back to the working end of the habitat and finish up.

The vertical sides went well. Most of the material could be applied by roller with only minor brushing of the rougher patches. They'd paint those first with a brush to layer on some material, and then a roller would smooth things out. The finish looked surprisingly good. We were about three hours in when we started to attack the flat areas. The patches were larger and had more rough areas. The big positive was we had gravity on our side. The Aquatapoxy flowed better and seemed to settle smoother. Both crew members with brushes painted the pitted area liberally, and the roller guys followed up and leveled things out, leaving an acceptably smooth finish. The work continued for just over two more hours. Took less time then we figured, must have been gravity...

The fans were blowing all the while, and the topsides were well underway to setting up. The bottom would take a bit longer. Steve recommended we try to get to four o'clock and then check the bottom of the habitat. We let the trainers know our plan. They said the dolphins were doing much better on this shift. I would hope so. The only noise was the fans and the mixers for the Aquatapoxy. Compared to grinders and needle guns, the noise level was much less and better tolerated by the dolphins. Great news! Maybe they'd return to normal faster than we thought.

At four o'clock, we asked Steve to check things out. I followed behind and took photos. I'd been documenting the work from the start and had a good collection of before, during and after pics to develop a completion report for the Aquarium to use as a part of their compliance requirement. Steve said the sides were well set up and doubted there would be any issues. The bottom was set up with the skin factor acceptable in his estimation. I wasn't as confident as Steve. The areas with the deepest pitting and layer of epoxy paint were dry to the touch, but when you depressed the surface, there was give. Great, I could see it now, painted bottle nose dolphins. I was getting delirious.

Two all-nighters in a row was taking its toll. The whole crew was in the same shape. It was time to clean up and once again rollup everything to get out of there. It was Thursday morning.

We told Jimmy that we'd be back on Friday to get all our stuff out of there and sent the crew home. I drove my own vehicle and would stay a while when they refilled the tank. Steve recommended that this be done at a slower pace to not disrupt the finish. He wasn't worried about anything coming loose. I was just worried period; painted bottle nose Dolphins would be hard to explain.

There was no show planned for Thursday, so they waited until almost seven o'clock before beginning to refill the habitat tank. If the bottom filled without incident, I'd be happy and call it a night. By eight thirty, the bottom was covered and had nearly a foot of water. There was nothing but clear water. No paint or cloudiness to the water, and with the Aquatapoxy, there was no real issue with that whole nontoxic thing. We were done.

I'd sleep well, and if the dolphins ended up with painted noses, oh well, someone else would have to figure that out. I doubt the dolphins cared.

We'd have the crew regroup on Friday and clear everything out of the Aquarium before leaving for the week. Be a good chance to meet up with Jimmy and make sure the dolphins were okay. We all felt good about how we'd done.

Jimmy said the trainers returned the dolphins to their habitat without incident. They swam around, checking everything out but no painted noses as far as they could tell. They were eating normally, and the trainers were satisfied with how they adapted well. The shows would continue... soon.

Jimmy and the Board of Directors of the Aquarium now had everything they needed for the dolphin habitat to be compliant. We would provide them with a letter and report they needed within a week. They would pass their inspection, and the show would continue.

We'd be back again a couple of years later with Aquatapoxy. This time outside the hull on the bottom of the habitat barge and surveying to extend their drydocking cycle.

'Underwater Inspection in Lieu of Drydocking.' That would be right in our wheelhouse. We'd find out if you really can paint underwater. The Aquarium would pray that we could.

CHAPTER TWENTY

SEALAND – BAY SHIPBUILDING – STURGEON BAY, WISCONSIN – 1988

In 1988, Aquafacs had an opportunity to expand operational reach. The Great Lakes were about to be added to the bodies of water that we'd add to our service areas. Our client, Sea-Land, had contracted with Bay Shipbuilding in Sturgeon Bay, Wisconsin to build three new containerships, a rarity in those days.

The ships were designed to operate the Puget Sound to Alaska trade route and in that service, made them subject to the US Jones Act.

The Jones Act is a federal law that regulates maritime commerce in the United States. It requires goods shipped between U.S. ports to be transported on ships that are built, owned and operated by United States citizens or permanent residents.

The Jones Act required that the ships for Sea-Land's new route must be built in the US. It was good business for Bay Shipbuilding at the time, but shipbuilding in general had moved overseas. The last three Sea-Land ships were the exception to the rule and would provide much needed opportunity to the Sturgeon Bay community with great paying jobs while they built the ships. They finished the three vessels by March of 1988 and began the process for final acceptance and transfer to Sea-Land.

That transfer process was incredibly involved and included a number of underwater tasks prior to Sea-Land's final acceptance. Following the construction of each of the ships, they were launched and sat in layup at Bay Shipbuilders while they completed the construction and final fitting out of the ship. They were complex vessels and robustly built to handle the conditions of operating in Alaska and the Pacific Northwest.

Because the ships sat for a relatively long period in the water prior to the final hand off, Sea-Land required the hulls be swept clean, the propellers polished, and a video inspection of the hull and markings for the UWILD (under water inspection in lieu of drydocking) be completed. The video inspections would be the baseline to extend their drydocking intervals sometime in the future. All these things would be required prior to final acceptance. With a price tag of nearly two hundred million back in 1988, it was a big deal for both Sea-Land and Bay Shipbuilding.

We were asked by Sea-Land to take on completion of all the underwater requirements for their acceptance. Having earned their trust, they knew we would get everything they needed done and done right. It would be one of the last items for sign off for them before they could leave Sturgeon Bay and make their way out of the Great Lakes for that long journey to Seattle. They'd sail south in the Atlantic, pass through the Panama Canal, and then head north on the Pacific side to Seattle.

We had just the man to lead the project, George Osgood. His hard driving demeanor and experience made him the perfect choice. George had a top notch four-man team to do the diving and handle the underwater scope of work. He had managed crews with his Marblehead Steel Company for decades and had all the skills to succeed and a good sense of humor to work things out with crews. He'd been on a bunch of different diving jobs after joining Aquafacs and had a good handle on logistics and all the nuts and bolts that were required to support an ongoing diving operation. I was confident we had a great team. Sea-Land counted on it.

When the first of the Sea-Land ships was ready for us to begin the acceptance process, George led the team from Boston. I would attend but had separate logistics due to a scheduling conflict that delayed my departure. They would all fly into Green Bay and then head north to Sturgeon Bay to attend the ship at Bay Shipbuilding.

George and the crew arrived the day before I did and headed north to Sturgeon Bay. They needed to meet the ship and check the lay of the land. He had tracked down hotel accommodations and available air supply. We would use bottled air and a lot of it. George had it all planned out.

We'd need K cylinders of breathing air, 270 cubic feet of compressed air per cylinder. He seemed to have all the diving needs covered. I spoke to our lead diver for the project, Arne Backlund, the night before my departure to make sure they had everything and were comfortable heading out to Green Bay. If there was anything left behind, I could pack it and drag it along with me.

After being satisfied things were under control, I asked Arne how to find Sturgeon Bay. No GPS back in 1988.

Arnie said, "Get a map and follow the chicken bones."

"Chicken bones?" I asked.

"Yeah, chicken bones. George bought the biggest bucket of fried chicken I ever saw. We ate 'em all the way to Sturgeon Bay and threw the bones out the window. You should be able to follow those all the way to Sturgeon Bay. Not much out there but a two-lane road, open fields, and cows. Ought to be easy to spot all those bones." He chuckled.

"Very funny! I'll keep an eye out."

I spent the rest of the day before departure planning my schedule. I couldn't stay the entire time in Sturgeon Bay. I had to blow and go to Seattle. One of the APL containerships was inbound and due for propeller service. We had a guy out there with his own equipment and tender, so that was easy. Lining up the equipment to get the work done in Seattle was the challenge. We were short on tool heads, so I would travel to Seattle with the propeller polishing machine and 3M discs from Sturgeon Bay.

It was compact and we had a good shipping container that traveled as luggage, so not that big a deal. It was easy in 1988 to ship tools from point to point, but with my schedule, it would have to travel directly with me to Seattle. Arranging for the Bob Cat needed for the hydraulic power could be a crap shoot. There was no room for error on timing, so the equipment company had to be 100% reliable. The APL ship would only be there long enough to complete cargo operations. If we didn't make it on time for any reason, they weren't hanging around to wait on us.

I picked up my tickets for Green Bay and noticed it connected in Chicago, then on to Green Bay. Departing Green Bay for Seattle, my flight also connected in Chicago.

My return leg would be Seattle to Boston after completing the APL ship call. Bit of a run but seemed easy enough.

I had never been to Green Bay and was amazed when I landed at how small the airport and facilities were at the time. Green Bay, after all, home of the Packers, had always seemed much larger to me due to their storied history with the NFL. Turns out in 1988, it was a regional airport in size rather than a major one like Milwaukee. Oh well, we had to work with it.

After getting my rental car, I headed from Green Bay to Sturgeon Bay. I bought a map and enjoyed a great ride. Chicken bones aside, it was a picturesque route with open fields and rolling hills. Plenty of cows and as green as could be. The weather was mild in late spring. Great news for our crew. I did see a bone or two along the way. George's version of breadcrumbs, I guess.

I went directly to Bay Shipbuilding down on Third Ave in Sturgeon Bay and found the crew set up at the stern of the new ship and already working on the propeller. Good thing, as that was the tool I needed to take with me in a couple of days.

We weren't sure how long our scope of work would take, as one of the tasks was 'sweeping' the hull. That meant using a dual brush machine that cleaned a three-foot-wide track to remove any slime or growth that may have accumulated while the ship was laying alongside. Our hull cleaning machine used two hydraulic motors mounted to a stainless-steel carriage. The carriage was hinged with one motor on each side and a fiberglass floatation can covering each motor.

Exceptionally soft brushes much like you find on a floor cleaning machine were used to minimize damage to the new anti-fouling paint on the ship hull. The brushes were sixteen inches in diameter and worked in a counter rotating manner. That motion allowed for developing forward thrust of the cleaning machine and would propel the machine and drag a diver along at a rate better than two hundred feet per minute.

There was a lot of power for a small machine and good for building upper body strength for the diver/operator that had to ride the machine and direct the cleaning progress. Surprising how much area of the hull could be covered in a short amount of time. None the less, the new ship was large, and it would take a bunch of time to complete the hull. Figured I'd be long gone for Seattle before they got done with it.

The crew finished the propeller work on the first day and were on schedule to begin the hull sweep the next day. The plan would be to work from the stern of the ship where we were already staged and move forward from there to the bow.

Everything progressed well with the hull sweep until mid-afternoon when the diver called out frantically to kill the power on the machine. We blew a hydraulic motor, the one piece we didn't carry as spare. There had only been a couple of times when we had motor issues and had always been shaft seals, an easy fix. We had plenty of those.

Now what. There was no internet to google up a motor. The old-fashioned way, Yellow Pages, was all we had along with new friends at Bay Shipbuilding, to figure this out. There was a hydraulic supply house in Sturgeon Bay, no surprise with a large shipyard in the area. George called them to see what they had or where we could find a replacement motor. They didn't have anything we could use but said there was a large supply house in Chicago that probably did. He gave George the number and wished him luck, and luck he had, sort of. The good news is they had a replacement motor. The bad news was it was too late for FEDEX, so the motor wouldn't arrive for two days, unacceptable for our schedule.

George, being a problem solver like the rest of us, had a plan. He would hire a limo to drive him to Chicago overnight and be there when the supply house opened. He'd bring the blown motor with him to match up and buy the replacement motor. He would then fly back to Green Bay where we'd pick him up and run back to Sturgeon Bay.

If the plan worked, we could have the machine back in service by sometime after lunch the following day. Sounded crazy, but it could work. George could sleep in the limo on the way to Chicago and with flying back it just might not be that bad. Alrighty then, off he went.

My plan was to keep the crew busy on site and begin the video and photographic documentation we'd need to complete the follow up report. There was some minor fouling on the hull, but the visibility was excellent. All the hull markings were very easy to capture on video. There were no useable cell phones in 1988, so we could only hope George would succeed in his mission. He would leave a message at our hotel front desk with what flight he was on from Chicago to Green Bay. I'd send a runner to meet him.

I called the hotel at 9:00 a.m. to check for George's call. Sure enough, he'd picked up the motor and arranged a flight that would get him to Green Bay by noon. Way to go George! Our guy would be there waiting.

When he arrived back at the ship, the crew had already taken apart the machine and were ready to reassemble. They did a fantastic job, and the machine was back in the water before 3:00 p.m., tested and running, back in business again. They'd work a long shift to try to make up time. Truth is, we weren't far behind when you consider how much video and how many photographs we'd taken.

The next day was my departure day for Seattle. George was worried about the machine and wanted me to stand by as long as possible before heading to Green Bay. It was only a fifty-mile drive, but with check in, dropping off the rental car and dealing with the regional size facilities, left me concerned about getting out of there. There was no alternative itinerary that would get me to Seattle in time for the APL ship. So, I didn't have any flexibility here. George still insisted that I wait.

Watching the clock, I had to be on the way by noon, or I was not going to make it. At quarter past twelve, I blew out of Bay Shipbuilders and drove ninety miles an hour south to Green Bay. When I arrived at the front entrance, I jumped out, opened all four doors and the trunk, and dragged all my gear and personal luggage to the airline counter. The car was left with all four doors open and engine running. Once I checked in, I planned a quick drop of the rental car and on to Chicago.

When I got to the counter, the agent checked me in and handed me my boarding pass. I told her I had to return the rental car, and I'd be right back.

She said, "Mr. Lee, you have to exit the gate for the plane immediately or you will not make this flight. They hustled your baggage out there and are prepared for takeoff. If you don't leave right now, your baggage will arrive without you."

I looked back and could see my car sitting there out front, all four doors open and running. Oh, well... I asked them to let Avis know they had a car abandoned out front. It was still sitting there as we taxied out. That was as close a call as I ever had to catch a flight. It was also the first and last time I ever left a rental car running with all doors open and took off! Without me and the propeller tool head, that APL ship wasn't going to happen.

George would go on to complete the scope of work on the Sea-Land ship and came back a hero for saving the day with his trip to Chicago. He made sure they got all the video and photos needed to prepare our report. Great job! That would be my task when I returned from Seattle. That close call gave me plenty of story material to use in the future.

My Seattle trip was uneventful other than finally getting a chance, after the APL work, to hit happy hour for my first time in the world-famous Space Needle with the revolving restaurant and central lounge and bar. What a view.

Our APL ship had arrived on schedule. The work environment in Seattle was special and cold. With clear weather, the big sky vistas were amazing with Mount Rainier snowcapped and looming high above the landscape to the southeast of Seattle. I really enjoyed working out there.

The water was clean but cold, and the City was a great place to explore, with sea food that bested Boston in my opinion. King Crab fresh from Alaska and Pacific Northwest Salmon are impossible to beat. The people were friendly, and the city was inviting. No wonder it became a Mecca for the tech industry.

As for diving, the water never got much above fifty-five degrees in the summer or below forty-five in the winter. Quarter inch wet suits were a must.

We went on that day to execute our propeller work flawlessly. After I paid and thanked the crew, it was time for my final leg back to Boston. What a trip.

CHAPTER TWENTY-ONE

STANDING OVATION – BUZZARDS BAY

It was the last Sunday in November of 1988. I was sitting at home in Hamilton, Massachusetts, waiting for a Patriots football game to start. The phone rang. It was one of the Boston Harbor Pilots, our neighbors upstairs at Pier One. They got a call from a Tug and Barge Company out of New York. They had a tugboat that was towing a large fuel barge that became stranded in Buzzards Bay somewhere south of the Cape Cod Canal, and they needed help. Somehow, excess towing line had accidentally slipped over the side and got wound up in one of the tug's propellers and left them dead in the water in Buzzards Bay.

Buzzards Bay is a rough body of water, south of the Cape Cod Canal between Martha's Vineyard and the mainland. It was notorious for large seas and swift moving tidal currents. It was a real challenge to perform any underwater services offshore there. When I heard where the calamity was happening and looking at the clock, it gave me shivers thinking about it. This was going to be a tough one if we responded, not to mention missing the Patriots game.

When tugboats take barges under tow, they have special extra-long and extra-strong towing lines called hawsers. As they navigate a tow to clear port or coming into port, they pay out and take in the hawser to meet the conditions. A long length between the tug and barge is typical once underway to absorb the stress and weight of the barge they have under way. The line is typically large, braided nylon, often four inches in diameter or bigger.

When the line is stretched, and the tug is making way, it acts as a shock absorber between the tug and barge. Without that ability for the line to stretch, they could run the risk of parting the line, especially in bad sea conditions. That could result in a disaster at sea, environmental or physical damage to the tug or barge, or both.

The Boston Harbor Pilots had passed along a name and number for the dispatcher for the stranded tug. They had asked us to call them right away as this was a critical emergency. My lucky day, Sunday, Patriots game on, and I've got the call. I wondered later why I ever answered that phone. Surely, they could've found someone else... This was well ahead of cell phones or smart phones. So, when the phone rang, you answered it. Simple as that.

When we hung up, I called the dispatcher for the stranded tug and listened to the story. The tug had dropped an anchor after fouling the line well south in Buzzards Bay. They were headed north from Long Island toward Cape Cod Canal on a run to Boston when this occurred.

The tug was owned and operated by McAllister Towing. They were prepared to arrange for another tugboat to meet us south of the Cape Cod Canal at a location where we could load our gear, if we were able to help. I told him we were willing to give it a shot, but I had to make a couple of calls to line up help and logistics to get down there.

It would be better than a couple hour drive from Pier One in East Boston to the pickup point at the Canal, and

Hamilton was about an hour of Boston. I called Jay and let him know my Sunday was about to be ruined.

"Hey, it could be worth a few bucks, and it sounds like they're in a jam," he said.

Thanks Jay, always the accountant, I thought.

I called them back and told them we'd be on the way, but it would probably take until around five o'clock to get there, if we hurried. He agreed to have a tug standing by at the Canal.

Word was out. Somehow our fame at Aquafacs was growing. The tugboat operator must have heard that if anybody could help, it would be us, and we were out of Boston, not too far away. They called the Boston Harbor Pilots to track us down. Worth the shot.

If we were not able to assist, they would have to hand off the fuel barge to another tug to be towed to port or a local shipyard to get hauled out and free the line. We'd find out soon enough if they needed the shipyard.

I was able to reach my tender, Paul Mercaldi. He was just about as thrilled as I was. The weather was bad, really blowing, and that fine, misty sleet was spitting, the kind that could freeze you to the bone in no time. I scooped him up at his house in Beverly, and off we went to Pier One.

We would take the old motorhome to the Cape Cod Canal. It would be faster to load out and more comfortable, should we get stuck down there somehow. That water would be pretty chilly in late November. So, we brought a uni-suit, a dry suit made of quarter inch wetsuit material that you could dress in, wear long underwear, and zip it tight. Had to have it. Needed the jet fins as well.

The current in Buzzards Bay can rip with the changing of the tides. Two K cylinders should be enough air supply, so we threw those in the motorhome. We'd attach a regulator and rack the two together with a manifold to feed my umbilical hose.

My Superlight would keep me warm and comfy out there, I thought to myself. Nonsense, it was not going to be a pleasant outing. With that wind howling, the swells would be up and could be a hell of a ride just to get out there. I wouldn't be disappointed.

We left Pier One and headed south. Being Sunday with a Patriots game on, the traffic wasn't bad heading through the tunnel and south on the old expressway. This was long before the 'Big Dig.' A couple of hours later, we rolled up on the pickup location south of the canal. The tug was sitting there all lit up and waiting for us, just as the sunlight faded. It was a pretty big tug. Good thing, if we were going to be hanging around out there in the dark in Buzzards Bay.

The crew of the tug helped us load out the gear from the motorhome and then cast off heading south. They put the wood to it, but tugs are not speedboats, as just getting out there took two hours or more. Finally, off in the distance, I could see the bright lights of the stranded tug. The wind with the light rain felt like pins and needles. It was freezing cold as we approached the scene.

Our tug crew and Captain were great to work with. The Captain put on a pot of coffee, figuring I just might need a hot cup before tangling up, pun intended, with this mess.

Our tug finally came alongside, and the two boats rafted together. Once again, it was Showtime.

The Captain from the stranded tug came aboard, had a conversation with our Captain, and came by to wish us luck while I was dressing in. I thanked him. There was no real need to ask him what happened. It was freezing effing cold out on deck. I shiver to this day when thinking about it.

The place was really lit up out there, with both vessels providing high intensity lighting that could be a help once I got in the water and under the tug. The swell was running six to eight feet. Great. The stranded tug would lay pointed into the sea swell with the anchor down, so this was going to be quite a ride. I'd have to hang on somehow. Thank God my Superlight was a true hard hat. It would take a beating tonight with me in it. I had no doubt about it.

I asked Paul not to let out too much slack in my dive hose when we got started, but not too tight either. Didn't want that to get caught on anything and dragged around down there with that swell. I told the Captain that I didn't know what I'd find, but we've got great comms so don't go anywhere. We might need to have a conversation once we got into it.

I asked Paul to hand me a three-pound hammer. He asked why? I needed to test how tightly they had wrapped the line. If I hit it and it felt mushy, it would mean we might have a chance of unwrapping this somehow. If it was super tight, the hammer would hit hard and bounce right back at me. Well here goes. Down the ladder I went.

I wasn't disappointed. The swell was something special. The stern of the tug would ride up, and then whoosh, it would drive me down a good distance as it settled while I awaited the next swell. Hadn't hit my head yet. Timing the swell, I moved under and grabbed onto the hawser leading away from the tangle. Gave me something good to grab on to. That was the good news. The bad news was that the tug had two good sized propellers, and the port side wheel was completely balled up with less than three inches of the tips of the blades visible.

Time to see how tight things were. I gave the wraps a whack with the three-pounder. It was so tight the recoil from the hammer almost caused me to drop it. This was about as bad as it gets. With that tight of a tangle, I'd have to think about this one. I hung there blowing bubbles, thinking about what's next, when Paul came on the comms and asked, "What are you doing down there?"

"Blowing bubbles," I said. "The port wheel is wrapped up all the way to the tips."

"What are we going to do?" Paul asked.

"I'm coming up. Take up my slack."

There had to be a solution. As I was climbing the ladder to get back aboard our tug, I was staring right at a large winch they use for towing operations on our tugboat. Hmm, I wonder if we can use that? I had to speak to the Captain but had an idea that the winch might be just what we needed.

"Captain, can we use that winch to help me get that tangle unwrapped?" I asked, as he looked at me like I had three heads. "If we can use that, I may be able to take a back wrap on that tangle and have you guys take up on it until it rips it out of that cluster down there. If it pulls out, we simply repeat the action over and over until we pull free."

The Captain said, "Well I guess so. The hawser lead would be over the rail instead of in a chalk. If everybody stands back, it should be safe enough."

"Great, I'll get back in and give you guys direction to support what I'm cooking down there."

"Worth the try. Long ride to get this far," he said, not looking all that happy. "Not sure whether yanking on the rope would do anything more than draw the two tugs tighter together."

Back in the water, the swells weren't laying down any and seemed like they were growing. Great, I gave up watching a Patriots game for this? Oh, well. I had to time the swell again to get back underneath without the tug beating me over the head. I asked Paul to give me slack in the fouled hawser, so I'd have enough to back wrap the outer wrap. Once I had that, I said to go ahead and have the crew wrap their winch and let me know when they were ready to give it a pull.

Paul said, "We're ready."

"If this works it should come out of there like a shot. You should know when it pops out, and if it does pop, stop the winch so we can do it again. Keep your fingers crossed. OK suck it up."

I backed away not knowing what would happen but hoped it would pop. I could hear the sound of the winch straining and the two tugs getting sucked together as they drew down hard on the winch. Then, POW! It literally sounded like gun fire.

Paul got back on the coms sounding a little excited, "Did that pull free?"

Like a wise guy, I said, "You tell me. I was nowhere near it."

"We've got slack up here," he said.

"Guess it worked. Let's do that again."

POW came the second wrap. We kept going, one pow after another as we pulled each wrap out of the tangle. The outer tips of the blades were getting bigger and bigger.

Finally, the last few wraps were visible and appeared loose. I asked them to stop and let me unwrap the last of the wraps. They could take up the slack as it came loose. Last wrap, free at last! They pulled up the last of the hawser. We had untangled the whole line that was wrapped around the port propeller without damaging or cutting the hawser.

I asked Paul to take up my slack; I was coming out. When I unlatched my Superlight and took my helmet off, there were about twenty guys hanging off both tugs and the barge, clapping and cheering!

As it turns out, the Captain of the stranded tug was extremely popular, and everyone worried this might cost him his job. That line was over ten thousand feet long, one piece. No way to splice. That would mean replacement if it was cut or damaged and would cost a fortune. I laughed and waved to the crew.

I just wanted to get out of the weather and grab a hot coffee. Standing ovation... Never had one of those before for any diving work. God knows I probably earned a few along the way. It felt great that we were able to save the day for that Captain. It would be a long, cold ride back to the Cape Cod Canal and back to Boston. Paul was going to have to carry the load and drive us back to Pier One. I was beat. Those swells didn't help me any. Monday would be a day off, that much was for sure.

CHAPTER TWENTY-TWO

AQUAFACS - THE FINAL CHAPTER

There are hundreds of stories and adventures that still live in memory to be told. As for Aquafacs, from the meteoric rise, to the rebellion on the West Coast, and ultimately the internal struggles that would be the end of the dream, it was an extreme challenge.

With all the successes and financial rewards, it was a given that competition would arise, and our pricing challenged. The 'we dive deeper cheaper' crowd was catching on, and now that Aquafacs had made propeller polishing a matter of routine, the fee schedules were dropping. The fleetwide programs were under pressure. Even with our proven history and long track record of specialized services, we were under the gun.

The first nail in the coffin was when the west coast operation, led by Chris Provost, decided they needed to twist off and go it alone, stealing our APL fleet and developing other services and clients. They changed their name to A-PAC Marine, trying a clever disguise as an acronym for Aquafacs Pacific. Their rationale was that Aquafacs was not supplying enough support, and they were forced to make the change to salvage all the effort and good will they'd established with our prime client out west, American Presidents Line. The Aquafacs Partner group was outraged by their conduct and contemplated taking legal action.

Legal action was coming alright, but not against A-PAC. After years of commitment and sacrifice by the so-called Partners, Wilkerson flatly refused to grant and issue the common stock of Aquafacs. From the beginning, it was promised to all.

Not validating and rewarding the ownership stake of the 'partners' was the ultimate betrayal. In short, it was the end. It was all over with nothing left but the lawsuits. Sheer greed by Wilkerson, and now the fight. For what, the bones of Aquafacs? Did Charlie really think he could blow everyone off and still have a company left to run? Wasn't going to happen.

I was out of town on a ship call for BP, formerly Sohio, down in Galveston, when things blew up at Pier One. Jay had called and left a message at the hotel. When I called him back, he was home and really pissed.

Jay described, at length, the fight that happened earlier at the office when Charlie was confronted by Jay, George Osgood and Captain Bernie about their ownership position of Aquafacs. Wilkerson responded that he had no intention of issuing stock to any of the partners, as promised. He had gone on to incorporate Aquafacs, solely in his name, behind everyone's back. David Keefe and I were not around and spared the agony. What a mess.

Now what? We still had work needing to be done with Sea-Land, Maritime Overseas and Hess, to mention a few. No way Charlie was going to manage any of that. He had no base or established relationships that he could count on to continue as Aquafacs. It was going to take a bold move to save what we'd built from going down all together.

I spoke with Jay and David Keefe about ginning up a new venture and reaching out to our established client base. The explanation could be as simple as an organizational name change. We were going to move forward with our scheduled commitments. Nothing else would change other than the name. No need to air our laundry to the industry.

Jay and David liked the idea, but neither were willing to buy into the new deal. They'd be too busy suing Wilkerson, but if I wanted to give it a shot, they said have at it. David Keefe said he had an old corporate entity filed in Massachusetts that he'd be willing to sell me to make it an easy organizational change. With a name change and a little razzle dazzle, I just might be able to pull it off. This was a long time before the changes in Corporate Governance. At the time, we were able to work with a simple phone call commitment from the client, with a follow up work order for billing purposes. I had great personal relationships with Sea-Land and Maritime Overseas and steady work planned in St. Croix with Hess. If this worked, the only business change would be the work order being issued to the new company.

Time to act. I had to do this. A new name bubbled up for me while contemplating the importance of name recognition, Leeward Marine. Adding a bi-line, Technical Diving Services, the new adventure was named and ready to rock. Catchy name, the game was on. Puffin Inc. would become Leeward Marine.

Time to pick up the phone...

The new adventures will continue from the Caribbean to the Croatian war. A final sunset for AQUAFACS as LEEWARD MARINE would become MY PHOENIX.

ABOUT THE AUTHOR

    This book has been written entirely by Christopher Lee. At the time of first publishing in 2019, he is retired at age sixty-six and living in Sarasota, Florida. The events in this book are but a fraction of the stories he has to tell during the thirteen-year period from 1976 until part way through 1989. He spent ten of those years as a hard hat commercial diver. Having finished first in his class in early 1979 at Commercial Diving Center in Wilmington, California, he went on to a colorful career in Marine Construction and working closely with the Maritime Industry on large ships and Supertankers.

    The author tapped out of Commercial Diving in 1995 after a series of close calls on extremely dangerous projects in LA and St. Lucia in the Caribbean. After retiring from commercial diving, he went on to a new adventure, a twenty-two-year career building out the first PCS wireless network in Florida. As a Construction Engineer, he worked with a team in Tampa building the generations of technology that led to the latest smart phones now coming into focus in 2019 for Verizon Wireless.

Author, 1978 – Rare Photo - Pre-Diving School

REFERENCES

Horovitz, Bruce. "End Nigh in Huntington Beach Popular Pier Cafe Destroyed by '83 Storms to Reopen." *Los Angeles Times*, 20 Sept. 1985, https://www.huntingtonbeachca.gov/files/users/library/complete/071018-4.pdf.

Jarlson, Gary. "Gala for Old Love Beach Town Pier Is Back in Business ." *Los Angeles Times*, 22 Sept. 1985, https://www.huntingtonbeachca.gov/files/users/library/complete/071018-5.pdf.

"Lloyd's Register of Shipping." *Books Boxes & Boats Maritime & Historical Research*, http://www.maritimearchives.co.uk/lloyds-register.html.

Ryan, Mary. "Sealab II: Remembering the 'Tilton' Hilton' 50 Years Later." *The Sextant*, 1 Sept. 2015, https://usnhistory.navylive.dodlive.mil/2015/09/01/sealab-ii-remembering-the-tilton-hilton-50-years-later/.

Selsky, A. (1986, April 21). American, Four Hondurans Found Bound In Tegucigalpa Fire . *The Boston Globe*.

www.ingramcontent.com/pod-product-compliance
Lightning Source LLC
Chambersburg PA
CBHW061404160426
42811CB00114B/2375/J